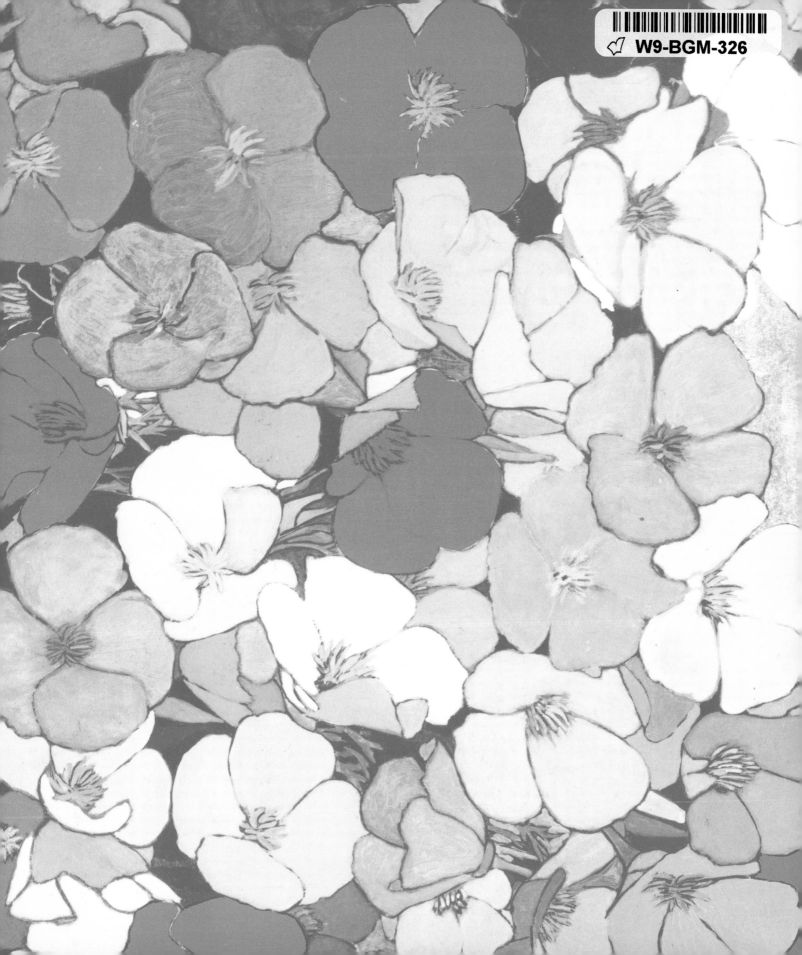

MATHEWS

MASTERPIECES OF THE
CALIFORNIA DECORATIVE STYLE

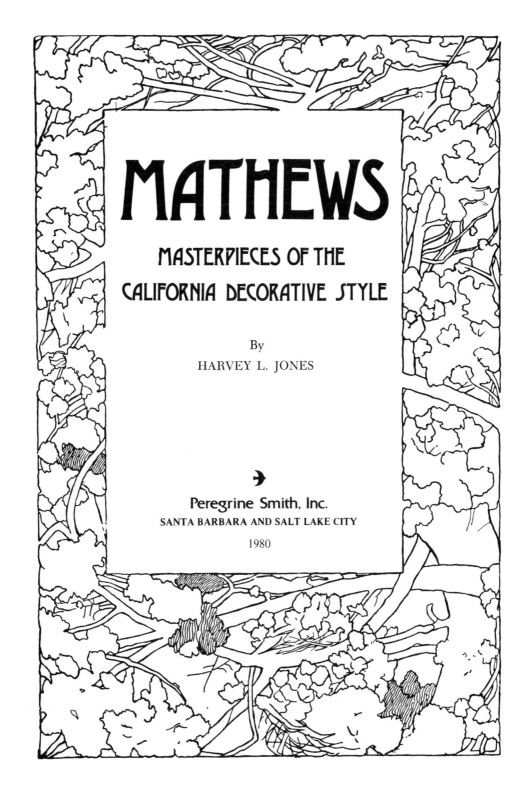

MATHEWS

MASTERPIECES OF THE
CALIFORNIA DECORATIVE STYLE

By

HARVEY L. JONES

Peregrine Smith, Inc.

SANTA BARBARA AND SALT LAKE CITY

1980

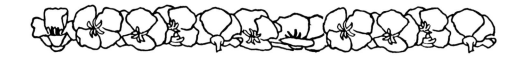

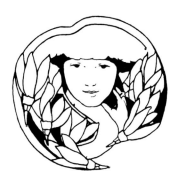

Initials and vignettes used in this book were designed by
Arthur and Lucia Mathews for *Philopolis* Magazine.

Book design and production by Harvey L. Jones and Richard A. Firmage.

Manufactured in the United States of America.

Front Cover Illustration:
Arthur F. Mathews, *Youth*

Back Cover Illustration:
Arthur F. Mathews, *Eve*

Endpaper:
Lucia K. Mathews, Box With Lid (detail)

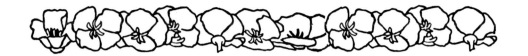

Contents

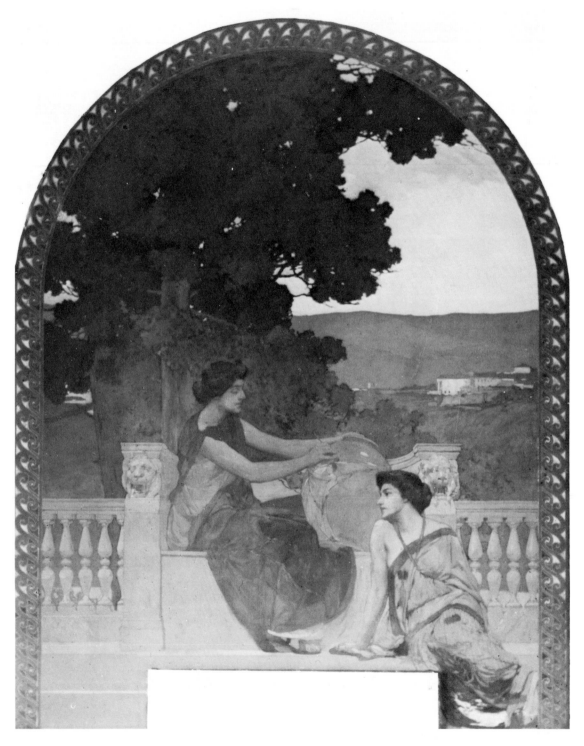

(cat. no. 83)
Arthur F. Mathews
The Arts, 1904

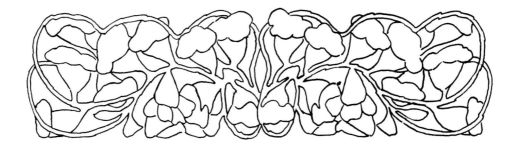

Foreword

In recent years, particularly since the celebration of the United States Bicentennial in 1976, Americans have increasingly shown an interest in the rediscovery of this nation's artistic heritage.

Attempts to determine what is characteristically American about American art have produced large quantities of newly researched material that has led to discoveries of previously overlooked artists and art styles or movements that occur within a larger regional or national context. In many instances the new information is first published in catalogues of exhibitions organized by museums that in turn serve to generate further research and more exhibitions.

Since 1972, when The Oakland Museum mounted the first retrospective survey ever assembled to show the extensive range of artistic expressions of Arthur F. Mathews and his wife, Lucia Kleinhans Mathews, there has been a rapidly growing appreciation for their works and an interest in establishing their rightful place in history among America's finest artists.

Most of the material for this book, gathered from the archives and collections of The Oakland Museum and from lenders to the exhibition, was originally published as a catalogue of the exhibition. At that time there had been no mention of either artist in the standard surveys of American art history or in major exhibition catalogues. Among the important collections of American art outside California, only the Metropolitan Museum of Art in New York listed a single Mathews work. Moreover, it was not until the national tour of the exhibition *Mathews: Masterpieces of the California Decorative Style* in 1973, that representative works by either artist had been seen beyond their home state in over fifty years.

That this remarkable couple should be the subject of rediscovery for Californians as well is even more surprising. Although Arthur and Lucia Mathews were among the most predominant and influential artists active in San Francisco from the 1890s through the 1920s, few of their stylish works had been shown publicly since then.

Three major artistic sensibilities enjoyed almost equal vogue in California at the turn of the century. The first was the spirit of what has recently been termed the American Renaissance, a period of classical eclecticism exemplified by the ideals of Italian Renaissance culture and civilization with its sources in the Greece and Rome of antiquity.

The second and more extensive influence upon creative expression in California at that time was the American Arts and Crafts Movement. It was here in this state that one of the fullest expressions of the ideals conveyed by William Morris and the British Arts and Crafts movement took hold.

The California Decorative Style of Arthur and Lucia Mathews embraced the salient features of both national movements and added a third and most significant element—that of a distinctive regional sense of place. The prevailing inspiration of the California landscape, the indigenous colors and the local informal lifestyle, combine with the art historicism and the craftsman ethos of the other two impulses to produce the comfortably elegant style that is uniquely Mathews.

Arthur Mathews embodied the concept of a Renaissance man of the arts perhaps more than any other artist in California, then or now. His was the dominant influence upon Bay Area art when California's diverse cultural identities were being consolidated at the turn of the century.

The circumstance of his pre-eminence was a major contributing factor leading to temporary obscurity in the intervening years before 1972. Subsequent generations of artists and patrons repudiated the traditional values of an art establishment they associated with Mathews. The ultimate irony is that in retrospect both Arthur and Lucia Mathews have become legitimately identified as California's first modern painters.

As the virtual rediscovery of Mathews' paintings, murals, frames, furniture, decorative objects and publications continues, their selected works have been successfully included in several nationally circulated exhibitions with a wide diversity of themes: California landscape painting, the American Arts and Crafts Movement, Symbolist painting in America, California painting and sculpture in the modern era, the American Renaissance, Post Impressionism in America and Turn-of-the-Century American art.

Happily, on the occasion of this publication of *Mathews: Masterpieces of the California Decorative Style*, the enduring appeal of these two artists seems assured.

Harvey L. Jones
June 1980

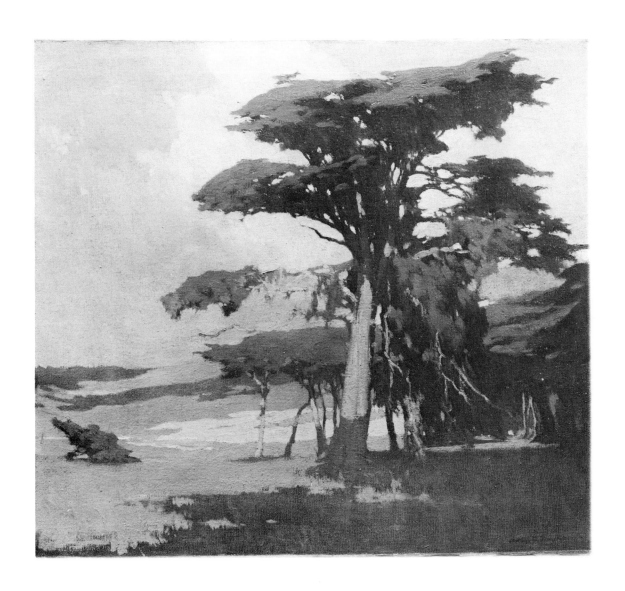

(cat. no. 25)
Arthur F. Mathews
Monterey Cypress, ca. 1904

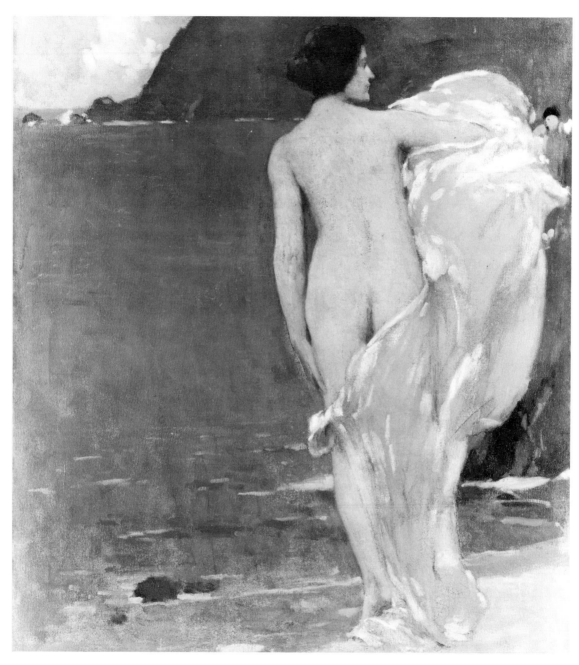

(cat. no. 36)
Arthur F. Mathews
Water Queen

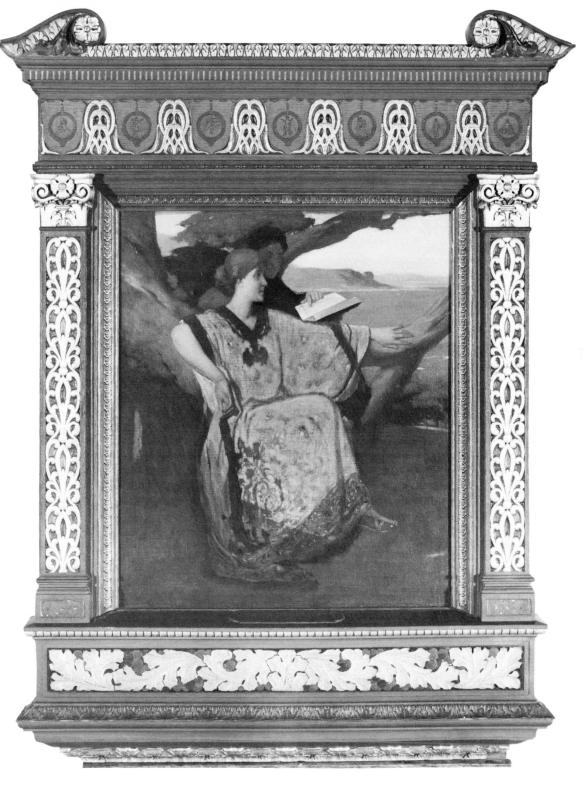

(cat. no. 27)
Arthur F. Mathews
California, 1905

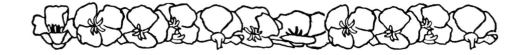

ARTHUR F. MATHEWS
1860-1945

LUCIA KLEINHANS MATHEWS
1870-1955

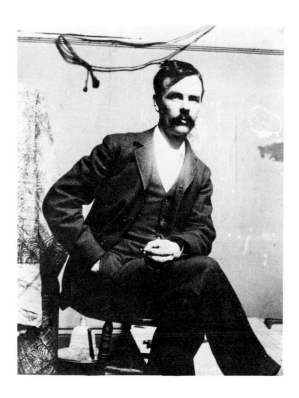

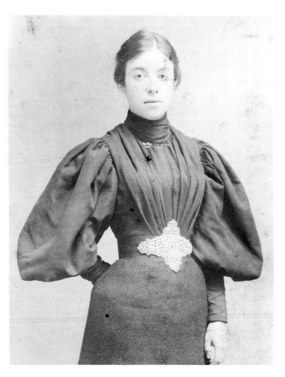

Arthur F. Mathews, ca. 1890

Lucia Kleinhans (Mathews) ca. 1890

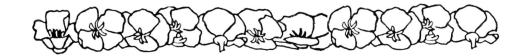

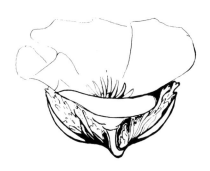

Biographical Chronology

1860   Arthur Frank Mathews, born October 1, in Markesan, Wisconsin; one of nine children (some of whom died in infancy) of Julius Case and Pauline Hope (McCracken) Mathews.

1866   Family left for California by ship from East Coast, crossing Panama Isthmus by train. Intended residency in Los Angeles terminated owing to experience of earthquake.

1867   Family settled in Oakland. Father, Julius, established architectural offices which AFM frequented during childhood. AFM entered local school. Early interest in drawing guided by individual lessons from Helen Tanner Brodt, Art Director for Oakland Public Schools.

1870   Lucia Kleinhans (pronounced Loo'-sha), born August 29, San Francisco, eldest of three children of John and Elizabeth (Ribble) Kleinhans. Father originally from New Jersey, sailed via Cape Horn to San Francisco some years earlier, established successful wholesale grocery business.

14

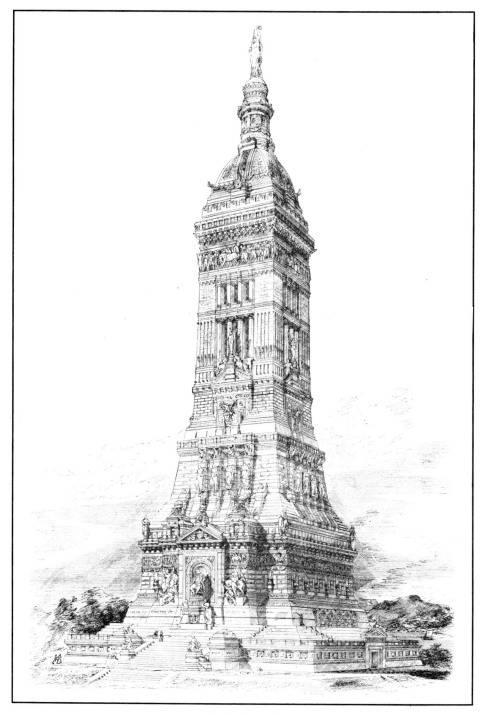

Arthur F. Mathews
Design for Washington Monument, 1879

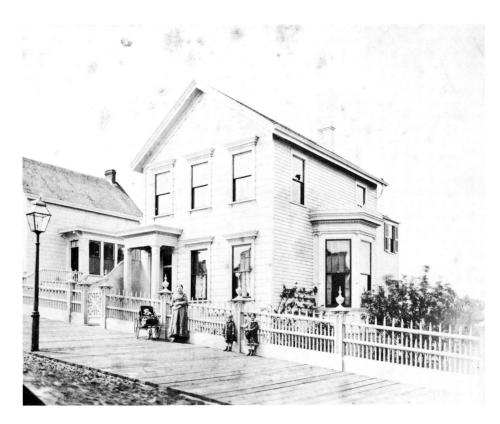

Kleinhans residence, 670 Fell Street, San Francisco, ca. 1878

1875	AFM entered four year apprenticeship as architectural draftsman at father's office. Older brother Walter J. Mathews active in profession locally and in Los Angeles; younger brother Edgar A. Mathews to begin practice in 1890's. AFM reportedly taken through 1880 as private pupil of Henry Bruen, now forgotten Oakland artist.
1878	Kleinhans family in residence at 670 Fell Street (now demolished). Lucia in public school. AFM submitted anonymous design for interior decoration of a vestibule to *American Architect and Building News,* Competition #5. Entry, titled "Hero," illustrated and given honorable mention in September 14 issue.
1879	AFM entered *Building News'* competition for design to complete the Washington Monument, unfinished since 1854 due to lack of funding and pressures from dissatisfied architects. Anonymous entry illustrated and given highest praise in November 8 issue, also *American Art Review,* 1880. None of the designs constructed.

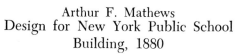

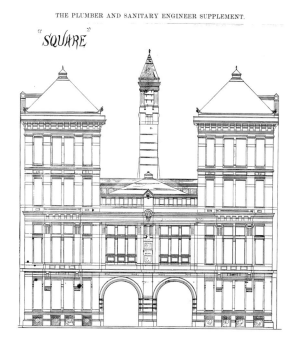

Arthur F. Mathews
Design for New York Public School
Building, 1880

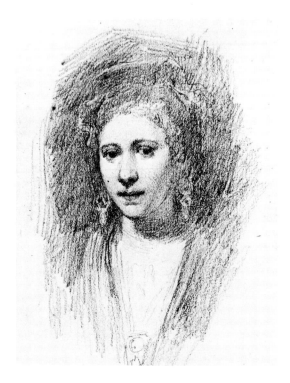

Arthur F. Mathews
Portrait Study of a Woman, 1885
(after Rembrandt)

1880	AFM won $250 first prize for design of model New York Public School building submitted to contest sponsor, *The Sanitary Engineer*. Entry illustrated and award announced in *Harper's Weekly*, March 13.
1881	AFM began three year position as designer and illustrator for Britton and Rey Lithography Company, San Francisco. Work included typographic design, illustration and ornamentation.
1884	AFM left Britton and Rey for free-lance illustration and design. Developed strong interest in painting. Worked to finance Paris art study. Reportedly helped found San Francisco Art Student's League.
1885	AFM in Paris through 1889. Entered Académie Julian, "little studios" annex in Saint-Denis. Studied under Gustave Boulanger and Jules Lefebvre. Soon established reputation as best American draftsman sent that year. Began one year study as private pupil of Boulanger.

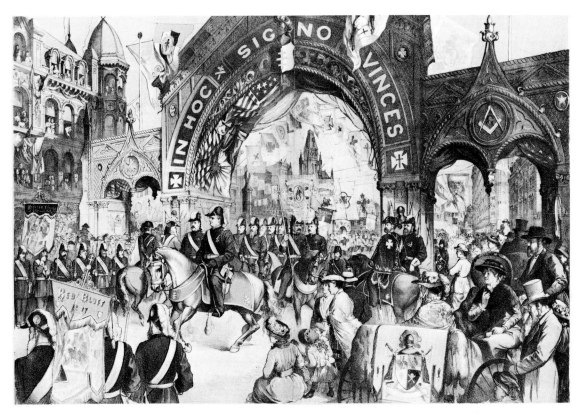

(cat. no. 57)
Arthur F. Mathews
The Knights Templar Parade In San Francisco, 1883

1886	AFM received Grand Gold Medal, Académie Julian, for distinction in three disciplines: composition, drawing and painting. First such medal awarded in nine years.
1887	AFM exhibited *Imogen and Arviragus, Portrait of a Gentleman*, Paris Salon. Travelled in summer months to Holland with a group of American students. Resided in a small village between Rotterdam and Dortrecht. Painted genre subjects.
1888	AFM exhibited Paris Salon.
1889	AFM exhibited *The Lilies of Midas*, Paris Salon. Exhibited *Pandora*, Exposition Universelle, Paris. Returned to San Francisco late summer. Taught life classes at San Francisco Art Student's League. Soon after, joined faculty at California School of Design as chief assistant to Director, Raymond Yelland. Taught life classes and advanced drawing. AFM showed first works locally at School of Design exhibition.

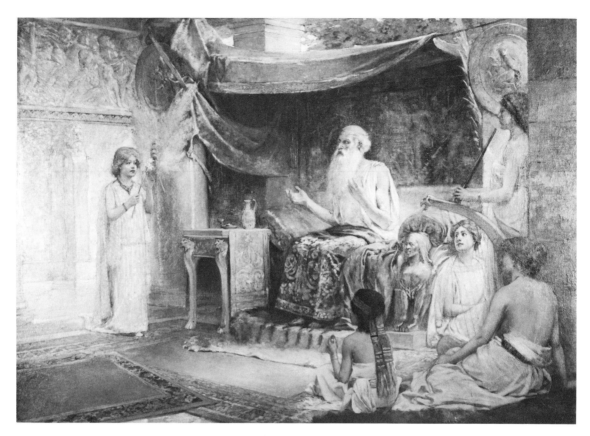

(cat. no. 7)
Arthur F. Mathews
The Lilies of Midas

1890   AFM held first gallery exhibition, Vickery's Gallery, San Francisco.

AFM appointed Director, California School of Design, shortly after Yelland's resignation. Retained post until April, 1906. Among the major reforms and changes in curriculum over this period were: de-emphasis of "antique" classes, in which students were required to draw the human figure from plaster casts of classical statuary; with this, an increased number of life classes, employing the nude or draped model in segregated men's and women's classes; inauguration of an artistic anatomy class; a teacher's schedule requiring their presence only two days a week, as in the Julian, to provide the necessary time for their own creative development, thus enhancing the quality of teaching; correlatively, encouragement of an independent but highly self-disciplined approach in student work, the abuse of which often resulted in harsh, critical hours. Students were encouraged to study in Paris, which served to create a close relationship

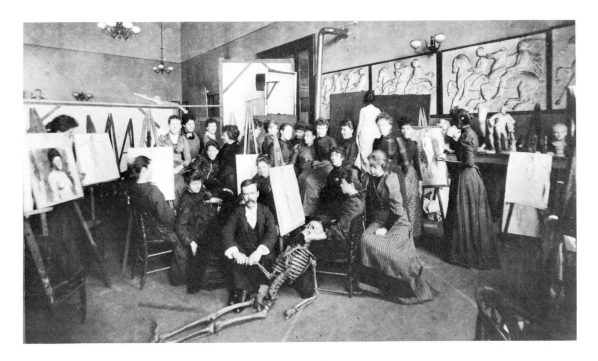

Arthur F. Mathews and women's life class,
California School of Design, San Francisco

with the Académie Julian as well as awareness of European developments. Among Mathews' students to achieve considerable fame in California were Francis McComas, Gottardo Piazzoni, Carl Armin Hansen, Ralph Stackpole, and Xavier Martinez.

1892   Lucia Kleinhans enrolled at Mills College, Oakland, for academic year 1892-93.
Lucia Kleinhans withdrew from Mills College before graduating, owing to father's financial reverses from mining speculation.

1893   California School of Design and Art Association awarded affiliation with the University of California and use of Mark Hopkins residence on Nob Hill through beneficence of Hopkins family. School moved in March and renamed Mark Hopkins Institute of Art.
AFM reportedly produced some 130 outdoor sketches and studies for large canvas, *Picnic at El Campo* (presumed lost).
Exhibited works in Fine Arts and California State Building, World's Columbian Exposition, Chicago. Around this time began regular showings at members' exhibitions of Bohemian Club.
Lucia Kleinhans enrolled at Mark Hopkins Institute of Art.

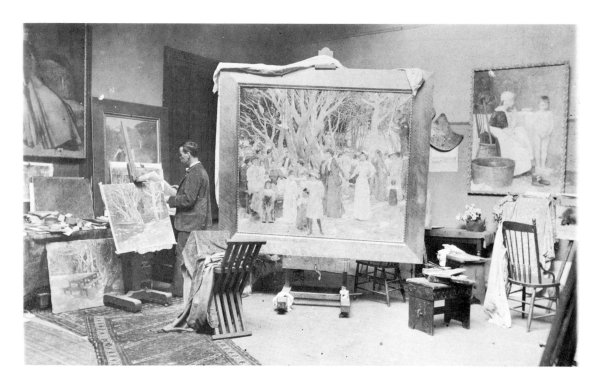

Arthur Mathews in his studio, ca. 1893

1894   AFM member of Art Jury, California Midwinter International Exposition, San Francisco.
Arthur F. Mathews married Lucia Kleinhans in small June ceremony at Fell Street home of Lucia's parents. Spent summer honeymoon in Santa Barbara. San Francisco residence at 508 Webster St.

1896   AFM and LKM exhibited at Mark Hopkins Spring Exhibition.
AFM studio at 728 Montgomery St., a complex which also housed working quarters of other prominent artists.
LKM worked at studio near Kleinhans home. Exhibited at Mechanics Institute's 29th Annual Exhibition.
AFM won James D. Phelan Award ($800) first prize for historical painting in competition with William Keith and others for his work, *Discovery of San Francisco Bay by Portola*. AFM reportedly studied historical accounts and period costumes for depiction of event. Painting given to Art Association by competition's sponsor, Mayor Phelan, later U.S. Senator.
Executive his first decorative commission, mural frieze and decorations at Horace L. Hill residence, San Francisco. The house was demolished (the frieze was saved).

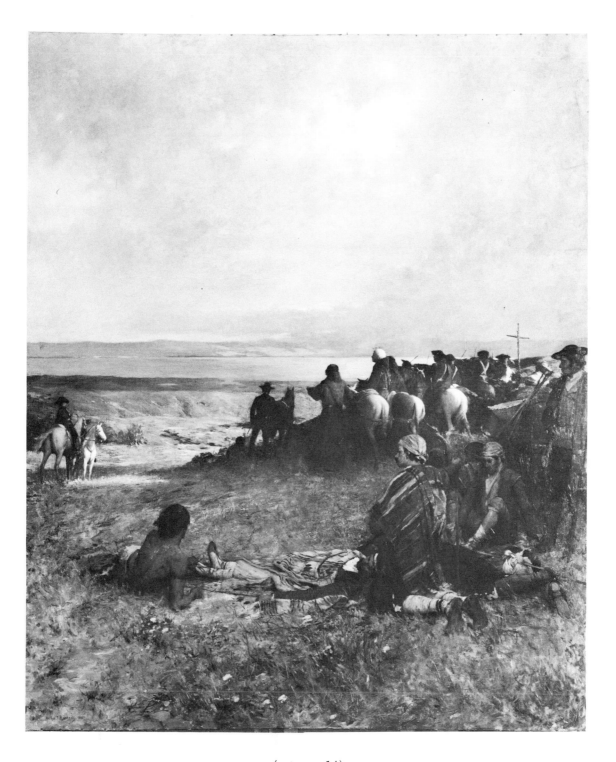

(cat. no. 14)
Arthur F. Mathews
Discovery of the Bay of San Francisco by Portola, 1896

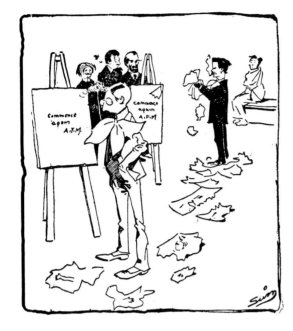

Cartoon by Swinnerton, ca. 1897
The San Francisco Examiner

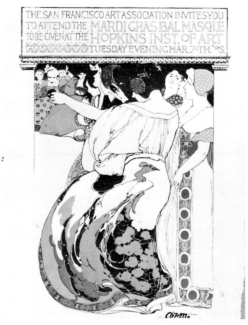

(cat. no. 68)
Arthur F. Mathews
Invitation for Mardi Gras Bal Masque,
Mark Hopkins Institute of Art, 1905

1897	AFM executed ceiling decoration, lunettes and piano decoration for drawing room of "Arbor Villa," Oakland residence (demolished) of Borax magnate, F. M. Smith. Brother, Walter J. Mathews, architect.
	Executed mural decorations, W. A. Dingee residence, San Francisco (presumed lost).
1898	AFM and LKM spent first part of year in preparation for European trip. AFM held one-man show, Mark Hopkins Institute. Exhibited drawings for Smith and Hill decorations, fifty oils, thirty pastels and a number of minor sketches and studies.
	AFM, LKM and artist friend Louise Schwamm left for Europe in June. First month spent in London, rest of summer in Paris. In Fall, toured Italy. Studied museums and monuments in Milan, Venice, Florence, Rome, and Pisa.
1899	AFM, LKM and friend returned to Paris in January. AFM opened small atelier, taught class in easel painting to small group of students. Reportedly exhibited *The First Sorrow* (presumed lost) at Paris Salon.
	LKM attended James McNeill Whistler's Académie-Carmen in a class of women students that included some Californians.

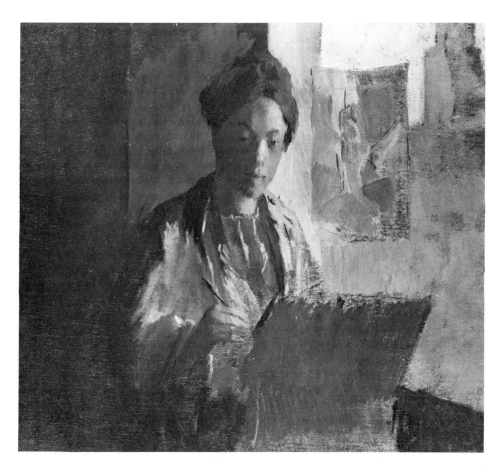

(cat. no. 101)
Lucia K. Mathews
Self Portrait, ca. 1899

AFK, LKM and friend returned to San Francisco in time for fall opening of Mark Hopkins Institute. AFM resumed teaching. He maintained studios at Institute and near home.

1902   Newly-formed California Society of Artists held exhibition in May, separate from Institute. The group claimed AFM's judging for school's shows biased. Also desired wider representation of artists, public recognition of progressive movements. Group included former students Gottardo Piazzoni, Xavier Martinez.

1903   AFM executed mural decoration (presumed lost) for music/living room in San Francisco residence of Rudolph J. Taussig, then President of the Mechanics' Institute.

1904   AFM completed and installed vestibule murals, Mechanics' Institute Library (destroyed in 1906 fire). Received commission for mural decorations in Oakland Free Library. Two completed panels, *Nature* and *The Arts*, exhibited at Mark Hopkins Institute.

1905   AFM held one-man show at Vickery's Gallery, first in five years.

1906   AFM completed cartoons (presumed lost) for tapestries, St. Francis Hotel. AFM and LKM exhibited Spring Exhibition, Mark Hopkins Institute, March 16-April 12.

Fire following April 18 earthquake destroyed AFM studio at Mark Hopkins Institute. AFM and LKM's works in private and public collections also lost.

AFM headed committee for distribution of relief funds to San Francisco artists. Funds raised through New York artists' auction sales and similar benefits by artists around country.

AFM designed 1717 California Street (now demolished). Construction completed October. Building housed AFM and William Keith studios, earliest in city's reconstruction. It also housed facilities for magazine and book publication, furniture production and sale. With financial backing and managerial assistance of partner, John Zeile, Mathews couple began multi-faceted project for the esthetic rehabilitation of San Francicso, in following ventures:

Philopolis Magazine, published monthly to September 1916, was oriented towards proposals in city planning and discussion of art. Various contributors were engaged.

AFM wrote and illustrated much of magazine, conceived and diagrammed city plans. LKM designed vignettes and decorative borders for magazine pages. Works of both reproduced liberally throughout publication.

Philopolis Press published more than a dozen titles to 1918 by authors of essays, poetry, books on art and California subjects. AFM and LKM designed layouts and decoration. Created special bindings for collectors' editions. Commercial printing included stationery, booklets and mailing cards bearing reproductions of Mathews paintings.

The *Furniture Shop* manufactured furniture, frames and decorative objects, all in wood, to 1920. Executed major commissions for domestic and commercial furniture and interior design. AFM headed the shop and designed bulk of its production, which required as many as 50 craftsmen. Thomas A. McGlynn was AFM's chief designer assistant. LKM collaborated on designs, supervised color selection and decorative carving. Also decorated tabletop items independently.

1907   AFM's position as Director of Institute formally terminated by The Institute's appointment of Theodore Wores.

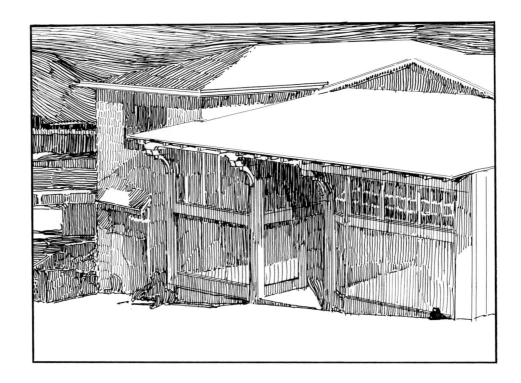

(cat. no. 71)
Arthur F. Mathews
1717 California Street

LKM helped reestablish The Sketch Club, a women artists' association, as major outlet for California artists' works. Served on Board of Directors, 1907-08 term.

Around this time AFM and LKM moved into the Kleinhans home, 670 Fell Street.

AFM became one of the founding members of Del Monte Art Gallery, Monterey. Showed at opening in April and subsequent exhibitions.

AFM completed two more panels, for Oakland Free Library, *Conquest* and *Resignation*.

1908   LKM served as President of The Sketch Club, 1908-09.

AFM on the selection jury. Both showed in The Sketch Club's Annual Exhibition.

AFM completed last two of six panels for the Oakland Free Library, *The Soil* and *The Grain*.

1909   AFM and LKM collaborated in design of curtain (presumed lost) for the Columbia Theatre (now Geary Theatre) in San Francisco.

AFM exhibited at The Sketch Club.

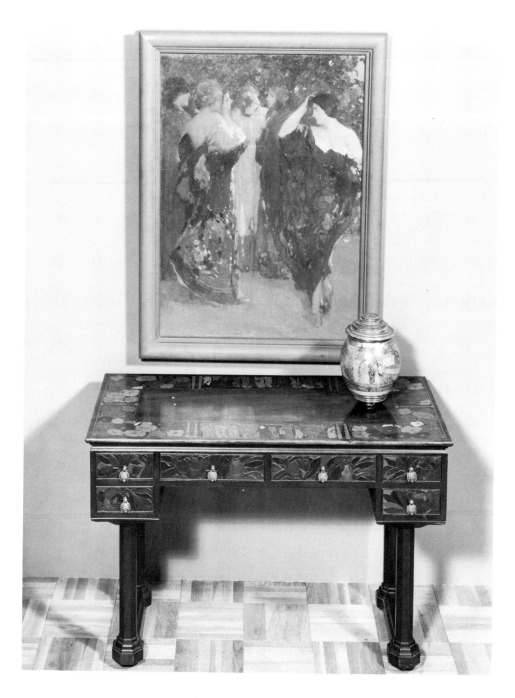

(Cat. nos. 34, 159, 30)
Objects by Furniture Shop
Arthur F. and Lucia K. Mathews

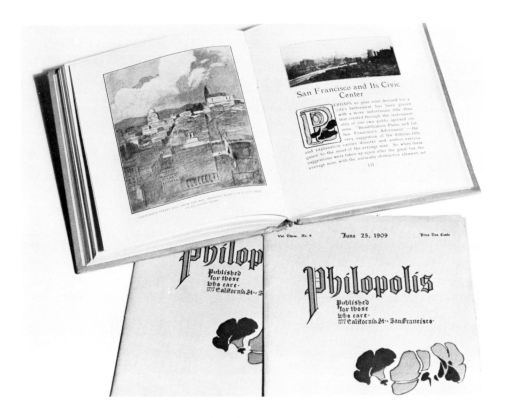

Philopolis magazines

1910	AFM and LKM began yearly visits to Monterey Peninsula.
1911	Furniture Shop commission received from Savings Union Bank, San Francisco, for interior decorations in Board of Directors Room. AFM painted mural, *St. Francis*, for Safe Deposit Lobby. AFM also designed bronze doors for structure: four relief panels depicted *The Indian, The Padre, The Miner,* and *Youth.*
1912	AFM executed mural panels, collectively titled *Health and the Arts,* for Lane Hospital Medical Library (now Pacific Medical Center, Health Sciences Library), San Francisco.
1913	AFM and LKM collaborated on the complete interior design and furnishing of the Masonic Temple, San Francisco. Sub-contract awarded to the Furniture Shop under Bliss and Faville, Architects. AFM executed mural (presumed lost) for Children's Hospital, San Francisco.
1914	AFM designed murals for State Capitol Building, Sacramento. History of California depicted in twelve panels.

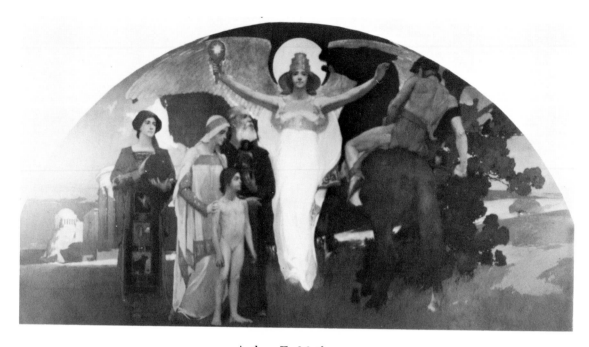

Arthur F. Mathews
The Victorious Spirit
Mural for the Panama-Pacific International Exposition

1915   AFM executed mural, *The Victorious Spirit*, for Palace of Education, Panama-Pacific International Exposition. Served as member of the International Jury of Awards, P.P.I.E. Exhibited 16 paintings, Palace of Fine Arts, in gallery shared by fellow juror, Francis McComas.
LKM exhibited watercolor *Monterey Pine*. Awarded Silver Medal.
AFM hosted dinner at 1717 California St. for colleagues from Paris student days, here for P.P.I.E. Among guests were A. Sterling Calder, William Merritt Chase, Frank Duveneck, Joseph Pennell, Edmond Tarbell, Edward Willis Redfield and J. Alden Weir.

1916   *Philopolis* printed last issue, September.

1917   AFM executed murals for Mechanics' Institute Library to replace those lost in 1906 fire.

1920   The Furniture Shop at 1717 California Street ceased production.
AFM worked in studios at Fell Street home and Montgomery Street complex.
LKM continued to design decorative accessories and keepsakes.

1921   AFM executed two murals for the "Catacombs" of Cypress Lawn Cemetery, Colma.

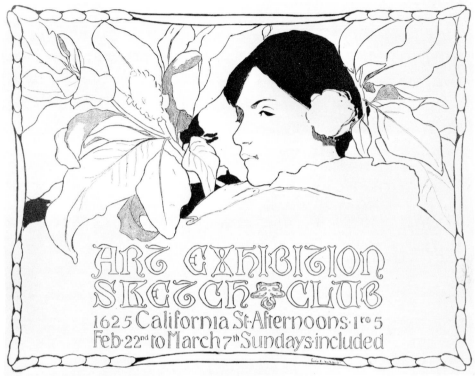

(cat. no. 120)
Lucia K. Mathews
Poster — Art Exhibition Sketch Club

1922	AFM and LKM collaborated on color scheme for interior of Alhambra Theatre, San Francisco.
	AFM executed murals for Curran Theatre, San Francisco.
	AFM designated to receive award by American Institute of Architects, Committee on Allied Arts, in recognition of his work in mural painting.
1923	AFM awarded Gold Medal for Distinguished Achievement in Painting by American Institute of Architects. Medal accepted on Mathews' behalf by A. J. Evers at A.I.A. 56th Annual Convention, Washington, D.C., in May.
1924	AFM executed mural *The Commonwealth* (presumed lost) for Supreme Court Chambers, California State Building, San Francisco.
1925	AFM designed stained glass window for Women's City Club, San Francisco.
1930's	AFM and LKM continued their production of oil paintings, watercolors and sketches, but in decreasing volume as the decade progressed.
	They continued periodic visits to Monterey. Painted last major landscapes.

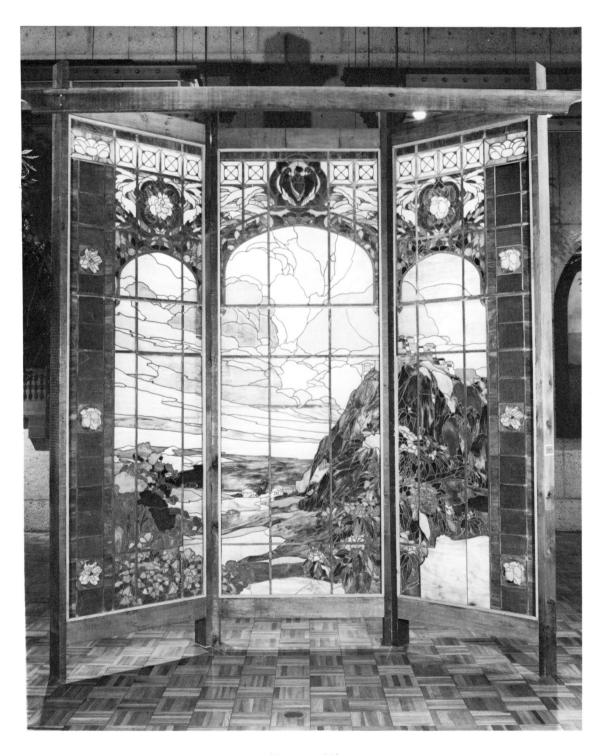

(Cat. no. 89)
Arthur F. Mathews
Franc Pierce Hammon Memorial Window, 1925

1934	AFM executed decorations and murals for St. Francis Hotel, San Francisco.
1935	AFM exhibited in California-Pacific Exposition, San Diego. AFM supervised conversion of old stable on Fell Street property into a studio. In later years he wrote a series of letters to editors of local papers. Also worked on unpublished manuscript, *Comedy Artistic*, a personal dissertation of esthetics. LKM sketched, painted and decorated small objects for personal use and for family and friends. Attended to AFM's health and affairs. She also remained an enthusiastic gardener.
1940	AFM and LKM exhibited in a show titled "California Art in Retrospect: 1850-1915," at the Golden Gate International Exposition.
1945	Arthur Frank Mathews died February 19, San Francisco.
1951	Around this time, LKM moved to sister's home in Los Angeles.
1955	Lucia Kleinhans Mathews died July 14, Los Angeles.

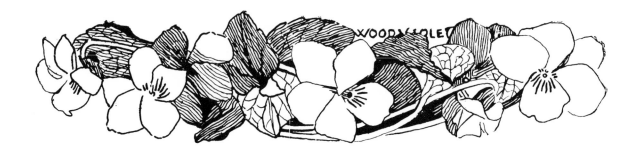

Mathews and the California Decorative Style

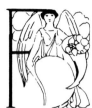OLLOWING the 1906 earthquake-fire, San Francisco's acknowledged master artist and teacher, Arthur F. Mathews, fulfilled the highest aspirations of a patronage interested in restoring their city to eminence in the time honored image. Mathews, as an artist, brought much more to this assumption of leadership than his credentials — nineteenth century values and a sound artistic training. He had combined his architectural background, French academic training, and the creative influences rife in Paris in 1880's to produce a style highly individual in its expression of original experience. The best creations of Arthur Mathews and those of his pupil and wife, Lucia Kleinhans Mathews, are in a style perhaps best identified as "California Decorative" and are worthy of the finest recognized masters of his period. Of the two, Arthur was clearly the dominant figure, not necessarily artistically, but by force of personality. That which characterizes his style was generally true of hers although she exerted her own particular accent within the style.

The practice of defining a regional style from the works of a small number of artists is questionable; to attempt such a definition from the products of one artist is to ignore the highly individual aspects of creativity crucial to art itself. Moreover, to suggest that such a style is a product of strictly causal elements in the artist's environment is to oversimplify. However, recognition of certain generalized tendencies can be useful in understanding the various forces that make up the stylistic identity of an artist or a regional art. The California Decorative style is a case in point.

During the transitional period between the aesthetic sensibilities of the nineteenth and twentieth centuries, when the arts were engaged in a re-examination of their critical values, San Francisco was dealing with an additional and still greater dilemma that followed the disaster of 1906. The raising of what was the West's city of art and culture out of the ashes of the great fire was an awesome undertaking that required confident leadership. That San Francisco emerged with its artistic spirit intact is significant, because the city was not rebuilt along strictly utilitarian lines.

The obvious dependency of the artist upon his patronage points to an important factor in the development of this style. The natural tendencies toward conservatism in times of insecurity were manifest in a patronage that preferred to rebuild San Francisco on models of traditional excellence rather than on the aesthetically experimental and unproven. The work of Arthur and Lucia Mathews exemplified many of the highest traditional or classical ideals of art.

Showing remarkable initiative in their individual and collaborative artistic production, they were a guiding and refining influence on the exuberant development of San Francisco's cultural identity in the years around the turn of the century. The demand for quality decorations during the post-fire period was responsible in certain respects for their emphasis on the "decorative."

IN painting, the Mathews' decorative quality also refers to the abstract significance of the design elements: line, color, form, and composition as they occur in the representation of ideas and objects. This notion echoing a certain "art for art's sake" concern was very much a part of Mathews' intellectual approach. For him, the word "decorative" carried with it none of the apologetic connotations of its contemporary use. Because of the consummate skill required to bring so many diverse components into harmony, Mathews was proud to consider himself a decorative artist in the sense that Puvis de Chavannes and James McNeill Whistler were decorative artists. Never before in California had so many excellent and diverse abilities in one man been brought to the service of architecture and interior design. His unfailing sense of environmental harmony extended beyond the pictorial boundaries of his paintings to include virtually all features of the urban *milieu*.

An inclination to place all aspects of decoration in a position subordinate to the function of mural painting can be seen in Mathews' color, form, and subject matter as well. He approached his arrangement of the formal elements from the orientation of an artichtect. In fact, architectural considerations were basic to his execution of murals and interior decorations. There is the subtle reminder that the depicted subject is at the same time an arrangement of color and form on a flat surface — the wall. Mathews' compositional emphasis was on the rhythmic linear development of forms in the arrangement of flat patterns or resultant shapes.

Not surprisingly, Mathews shared with many French artists of the late nineteenth century, an enthusiasm for Japanese prints. In his own way, he followed the widespread adoption of the Oriental methods of depicting three-dimensional space while maintaining the integrity of a flat surface. That Arthur Mathews also collected Japanese prints indicates a direct awareness of these principles; and that he employed the various devices with such subtlety and skill reveals an understanding of them beyond the superficial. He preferred to keep the illusion of three-dimensional effects to a relatively shallow space, parallel to the picture plane, a discipline especially appropriate to mural painting. But in Mathews' easel paintings, too, he remained aware of their ultimate placement in an architectural space. The frames he designed were decidedly architectural in concept and thus provided the transitional device that related the painting to its surroundings.

Arthur Mathews himself wrote that "Both Puvis de Chavannes and Whistler perhaps were essentially what this at times silly world calls decorative artists, for both could decorate a wall space without ruining its spaciousness or the room it enclosed." Mathews continued his observation of certain parallel concerns of Puvis de Chavannes and Whistler to suggest they shared the principle that "every painting must of necessity have a definite color note as a binding force in its construction."

Characteristic of Mathews' color was a general tendency toward closely harmonized relationships of hue and value accented by modulation of the color intensity. A method used by the Renaissance masters to achieve a harmonious transition between contrasting colors was to support the opposing hues with a brown undertone. Whistler and his followers substituted a cool grey tonality for the warm brown, which earned for him the derogatory title, "Apostle of the Grey." This title was later transferred to Mathews by a local art critic. Low key and close value colors of a dominant hue were fundamental to a late nineteenth-century American aestheticism referred to as "tonalism." It derived largely from Whistler's influential distaste for the coloristic freedom of Impressionism, and was widely practiced in this country. Aside from the decorative aspects of color tonalism, it conveyed a powerful sense of poetic mood and emotional impact. This appeal to the subjective in art took many different forms in the hands of various artists. For Mathews, it was employed to depict a mood of revery in his portraiture and atmospheric effects in his landscapes.

Nature was a primary source of inspiration for Mathews, but his landscapes offer a personal interpretation of the experience of nature rather than a realistic copy. In praise of Puvis de Chavannes and Whistler he said, "Neither was deceived for a moment by the prevalent notion that realism in art was the art, and neither ever conceived nature too base to study, nor so good that they should grovel in her abominations." On the same subject Mathews said, "The arts parallel nature or play at her; they only imitate in irony or illustration . . . the illustrator's art and the fine art of painting are two and separable."

His intellectual bias resulted in an idealistic art that favored the traditions of Greek classicism in spirit, although not in style. The Greek philosophy celebrated man's awakening from his natural environment. The concept of the *polis* (city) was a manifestation of this awakening of human values — of civilization. Greek art revealed an extraordinary sense of balance and harmony between man and nature. Emphasis was placed on the human figure through which abstract concepts could be expressed. Even nature "herself" was personified. This was the spirit, the ideal, the source to which Mathews constantly returned. Art and nature are conspicuous themes throughout his work.

Still-life or *genre* painting held little fascination for Mathews; usually he preferred the exalted conceptions of the academician. His subjects were often figures, usually female, which he placed in allegorical situations to symbolize a number of mythical characters or abstract virtues. The mythical characters, although most often drawn from Greek or Roman mythology, are only occasionally shown with their traditional specific attributes. Mathews seemed mainly to be interested in suggesting ties with classical themes rather than depicting them literally. In this respect, Mathews is further removed from the original sources than was Puvis de Chavannes. Among the various symbolic females in Mathews' paintings — spirits, goddesses, mothers, artists and personifications of nature — the most frequently used is the dancer. In this recurrent symbol he seems to combine most of the others — the spirit of freedom, aesthetics, virtue, femininity — in short, a nineteenth-century man's feminine ideal.

The relatively infrequent appearance of the male figure in Mathews' paintings suggests its inappropriate use in depicting the higher sensibilities of art and nature. Usually his male figures symbolize adventure, conquest, labor or authority.

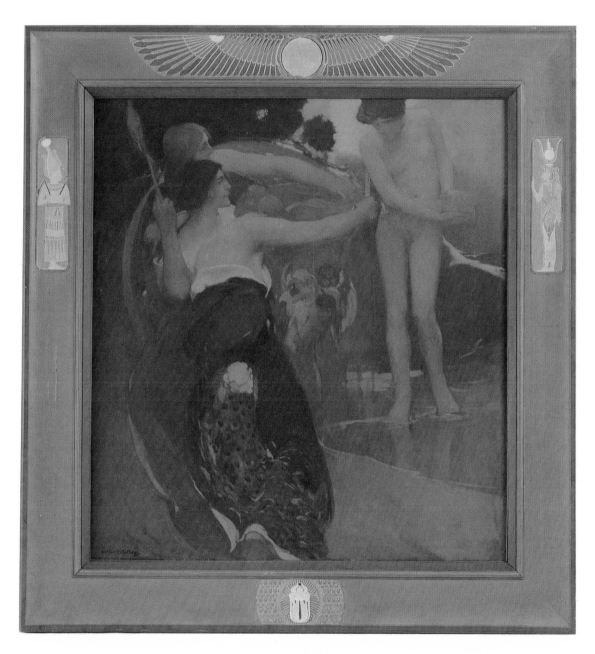

(cat. no. 31)
Arthur F. Mathews
Masque of Pandora

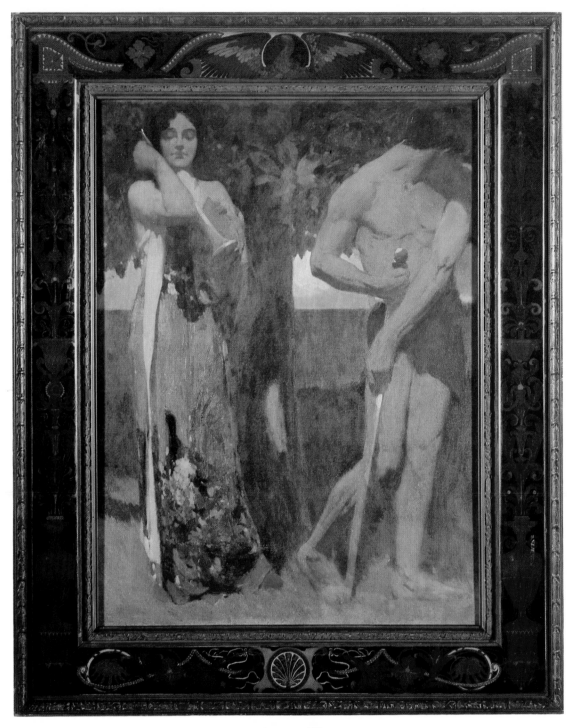

(cat. no. 35)
Arthur F. Mathews
I Piped But Ye Would Not Dance

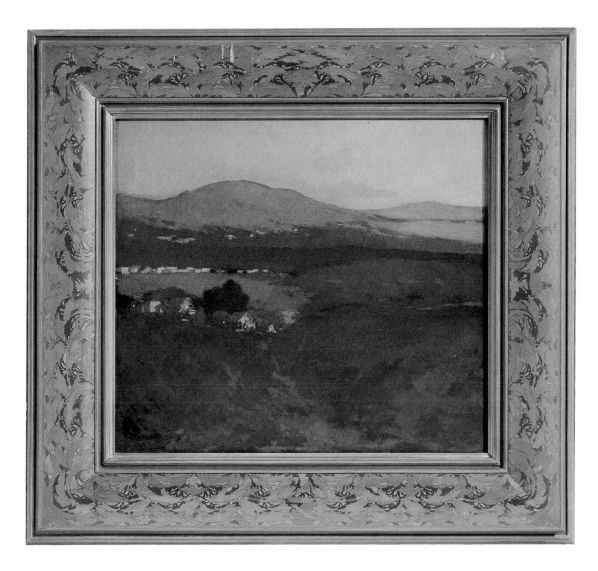

(cat. no. 51)
Arthur F. Mathews
Landscape—San Francisco

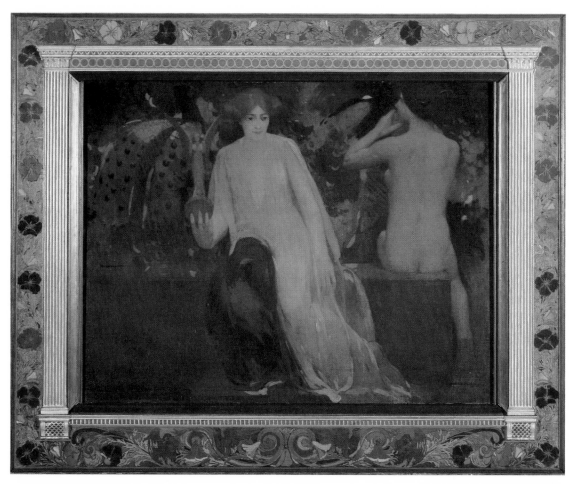

38

(cat. no. 32)
Arthur F. Mathews
Sacred and Profane Love

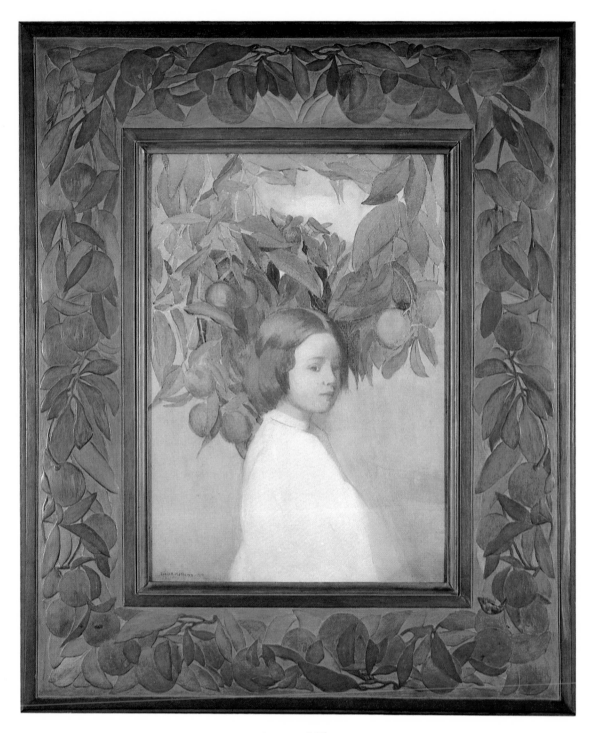

(cat. no. 123)
Lucia K. Mathews
Portrait of Red-Haired Girl

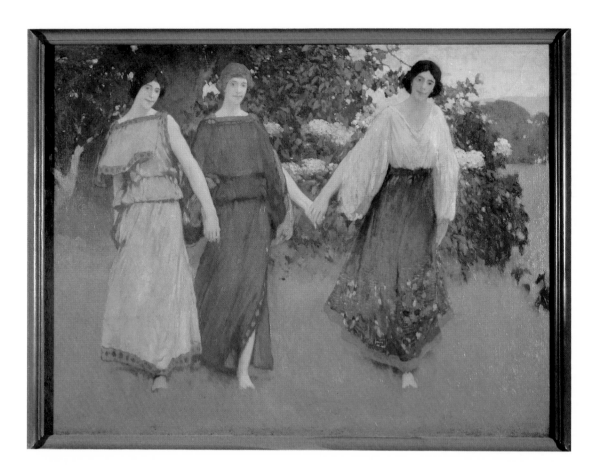

(cat. no. 40)
Arthur F. Mathews
Dancing Girls

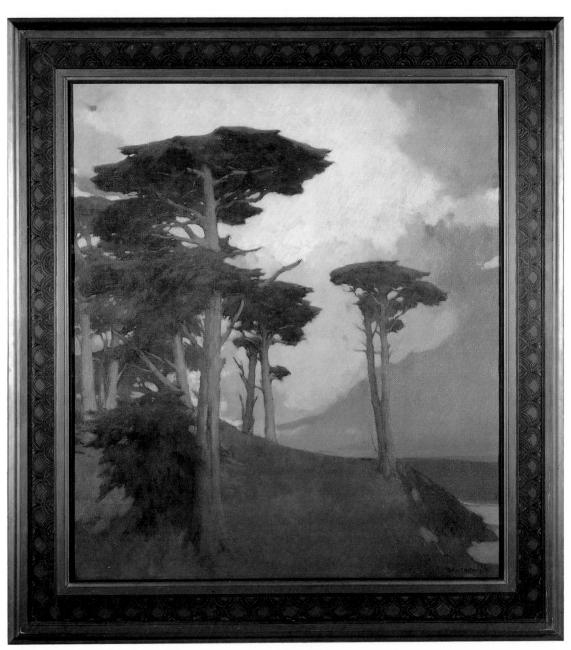

(cat. no. 56)
Arthur F. Mathews
Monterey Cypress #3, 1933

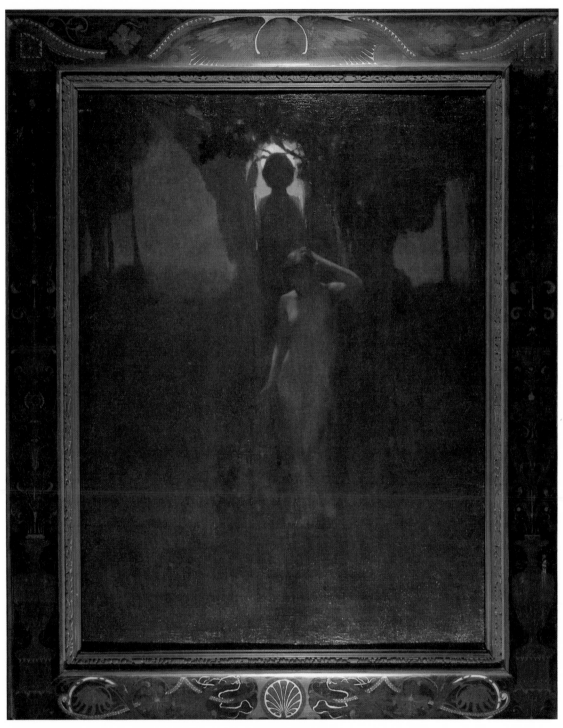

(cat. no. 8)
Arthur F. Mathews
Eve

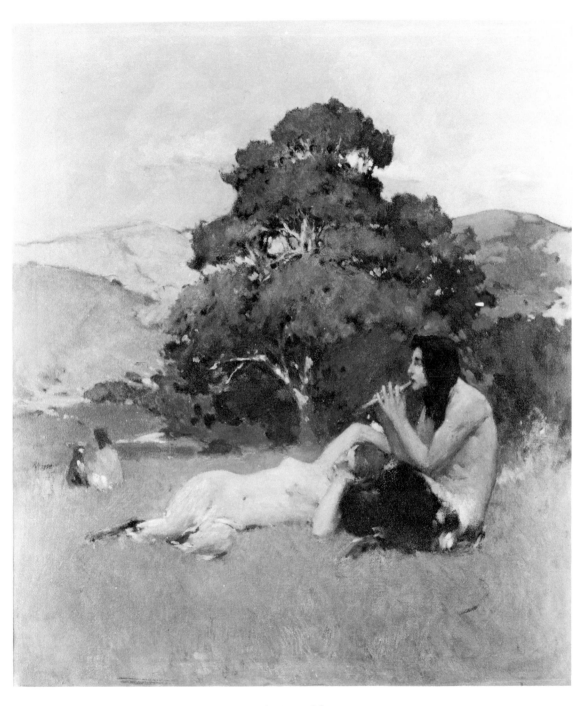

(cat. no. 44)
Arthur F. Mathews
Satyr and Nymph

44

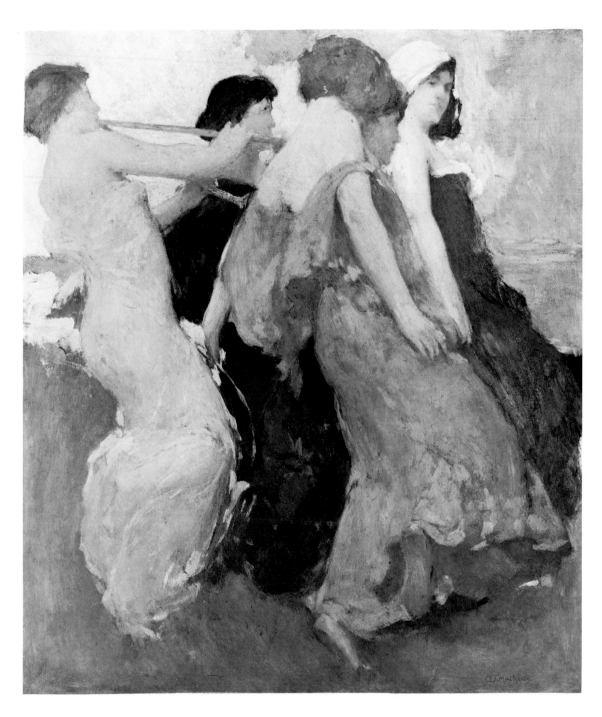

(cat. no. 41)
Arthur F. Mathews
The Dancers

THE appropriateness of Grecian themes in California art and architecture is not as unlikely as it might first appear. The flowering of the Greek revival in California at the turn of the century was manifested in several aspects of American life. Great interest had grown out of archaelogical excavations in Greece during the nineteenth century. At a time when America was turning away from frontier economics, Victorian industrialism and restrictive morality, its romanticized interpretation of the ancient Greek societies provided an ideal model for a balanced environment. Artifacts, sculpture and architectural fragments appeared on the scene in the form of plaster casts. Casts such as these formed the base of academic training in art at the School of Design in San Francisco. These suggested a life style based on the elevation of the arts, educational ideals, and importance of physical culture. Athletic figures in Greek sculpture and the revival of the Olympic games in 1896 inspired a "health movement" in this country. Some of the resultant effects were exercise classes in schools and the adoption of more "healthful" clothing, especially for women, in the form of loose-fitting "Grecian" garments. Moreover, the pastoral societies of ancient Greece suggested the healthfulness of outdoor living and gave rise to a turn-of-the-century architectural phenomenon—the open air sleeping porch. It was found to be especially agreeable to the mild "Mediterranean" climate of coastal California.

All of the arts were called upon for this elevated life style which seemed so appropriate to a nation devoted to the ideals of the original "great democracy." Physical exercise (calisthenics) for women was transformed into a dance idiom made world famous by such personalities as Isadora Duncan and Loie Fuller. The popular forms of "Greek Dancing" were based upon figures depicted on the classical Greek friezes and vase paintings. The poses were imitated and connected by transitional movements from one position to another, thus creating a kind of dance. These various peculiar Greek phenomena in the California environment are vividly apparent in most of Mathews' figurative paintings.

Concurrent with the romantic concepts of the Greek revival in California was another popular idea that virtually became a movement elsewhere as well. A dominant theme of the period was that of unity in the arts and it found its medium of expression in a style best known as *L'Art Nouveau*. It had its origins in the Pre-Raphaelite and the Arts and Crafts movement in England during the 1870's and 1880's and by 1900 had made its sensational swirl through Europe and America.

The term *L'Art Nouveau* usually refers to architecture and the applied arts. However, in painting, too, there was a certain *fin-de-siècle* involvement with exotic plant forms, aesthetic animals and precious womanhood rooted in *L'Art Nouveau* style. Certain aspects of this sensibility are reflected in Mathews' production. Mathews considered *L'Art Nouveau* merely a mannerism or fad, and not a style at all. It is unlikely that he consciously worked in the style; however, an affinity exists in his predilection for the decorative subject matter of *L'Art Nouveau*. Many of the larger themes of the movement were compatible with his own "art and nature" ideas.

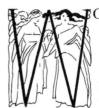OMEN became a symbol in *L'Art Nouveau* that reflected the period's aesthetic and exotic inclinations. This romantic concept of women took various forms: the Pre-Raphaelite woman was melancholy and languidly sensual, *L'Art Nouveau* woman was exotic and sometimes more than slightly erotic. The Oriental woman also contributed certain exotic characteristics that influenced the style. The decorative robes that frequently adorned *fin-de-siècle* womanhood in art are traceable to Japanese prints. The typical Mathews woman embodies only a few of the aforementioned endowments. Although she remains to an extent a decorative feature in his paintings, she generally symbolizes some abstract concept. Instead of the sensual attraction of women in *L'Art Nouveau*, we see the classical Greek impassivity. Her exotic attributes are limited chiefly to the clothing which is in itself symbolic of art.

In Mathews' paintings, women seem to be the personification of aesthetics, and its attributes are expressed by the depiction of nature's aesthetic creatures on her garments. The symbols for *L'Art Nouveau* movement are the peacock, the swan, and the lily, all chosen for their natural grace and curvilinear forms. When Mathews employed these symbols he maintained the naturalness of forms to a greater extent than did *L'Art Nouveau* artists. The extreme stylization and conventionalization expressed by the whiplash curves and arabesques of that movement are seldom seen in Mathews' work. The graphic designs, vignettes and initials Mathews used in his periodicals and book designs come closest to the style; however, the furniture, frames, and decorative objects show very little relation to *L'Art Nouveau* beyond the spirit of its origins. Here again the naturalistic representation of figures, flowers, animals and landscape prevails and forms the distinction.

Equally important to Mathews' style is the California landscape. The California landscape is truly distinctive in its contours, coloring, foliage and atmosphere. Arthur Mathews was frequently asked why an artist of his remarkable ability should prefer San Francisco to the art centers of the Eastern seaboard or those of Europe. "Why do I stay in California?" he asked, "California is an undiscovered country for the painter. It hasn't been touched. The forms and colors of our countryside haven't begun to yield their secrets . . ." Mathews was certainly not unaware of the many fine artists who had painted in California but rather he felt that few had really extracted what was essentially Californian in the landscape. He compared San Francisco and coastal California with Venice for its physical atmosphere. San Francisco's bright hazy sunlight he found comparable to that of the Adriatic coast. Culturally, he compared the touch of the Orient common to both cities. The source of some of Mathews' typically California color and light effects is suggested by his statement that: "I never work outside until after 4 o'clock in the afternoon . . . for to me the most extraordinary color effects that we find here in the West come only in the diffused afternoon lights."

Mathews' frequent visits to the Monterey peninsula reveal the source of other favorite subjects in his paintings. The pines, the

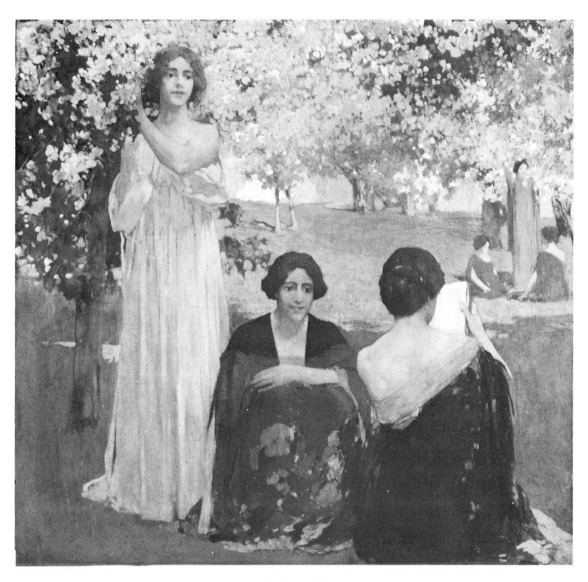

(cat. no. 46)
Arthur F. Mathews
Ladies on the Grass

cypress and the coastal oaks frequently appear in his landscapes and in the background of many murals and figurative paintings. The tawny gold of California's summer hillsides and a glimpse of the sea beyond is characteristic of the Mathews style. Occasional views of urban scenery in his paintings consistently reflect the typical local architectutre in both color. and style.

The mood of Mathews' paintings, whether portrait, figurative or landscape, is typically quiet and serene. The mood of revery in his portrait studies recalls that of Whistler.

The figures in Mathews' paintings maintain the passive mood of classical Greek sculpture and seldom break through the picture plane to engage one emotionally. The viewer remains a spectator rather than a participant, a concept especially appropriate to the decorative function of painting. The Mathews' landscapes, as well, maintain a quiet mood. Never does he indulge in the tumultuous storms and dramatic aberrations of nature that absorbed many 19th century artists.

The Parisian environment of the late 1880's was rich in potentially influential material for a developing artist. Various radical departures from traditional approaches in the arts included the Symbolist writers Mallarmé and Verlaine, the Impressionists, Cézanne, Whistler and perhaps very significant for Mathews, the indirect influence of Paul Gauguin. Paul Sérusier, an avid follower of Gauguin, was elected *massier* or student overseer of the "little studios" of the Académie Julian where Mathews was a student under the masters Lefebvre and Boulanger. In 1888 Sérusier met Gauguin at Pont Aven and painted a small landscape on a wood panel under his guidance. Gauguin advised Sérusier not to copy nature directly as he saw it, but rather to represent it transmuted into vivid colors with emphasis upon simple arabesques for the pleasure of the eye. When Sérusier returned from Pont Aven he brought the advice of Gauguin to a group of his friends at the Julian that included Denis, Bonnard, Vuillard, and Vallotton. The small landscape he painted for Gauguin later became the "talisman" of the *Nabis* group. That Arthur Mathews would have seen the talisman at the Julian and the works of Gauguin

in Paris is likely, and suggests certain sources, aside from color, for his own "decorative" style. Although Mathews doesn't seem to have mentioned Gaugin or even the French artists who were at the Académie Julian during his student days, his general reluctance to admit influences may be the reason. However, his paintings immediately after 1888, other than portraits, suggest some contact with Gauguin and also something of the Symbolist influence.

Mathews once wrote, "All artists are influenced. A school in the true sense is a series of counter influences—a system of active and reactive forces which brings forward a central or dominant quality." He felt that influences are only a reflection of environment and are modified by the artist's practice in his studio.

There were a number of European and American artists contemporary with Mathews who may be said to have been similarly influenced. The classical figures, the allegories and the murals suggest Puvis de Chavannes; the Mathews women call to mind those of Albert Moore or Whistler; the dancing figures are reminiscent of Robert Blum or Thomas Dewing; and the involvement with decoration, furniture and stained glass invokes the names of John LaFarge or Frank Brangwyn among others. Whatever the combination of influences and environmental experiences, they passed through the highly intelligent and finely organized sensibility of Arthur Mathews to emerge in the distinctive style we have referred to as "California Decorative." The style was not named by him, for he rejected the concept of stylistic identification as many artists do, but it originated largely in his work and that of his wife Lucia.

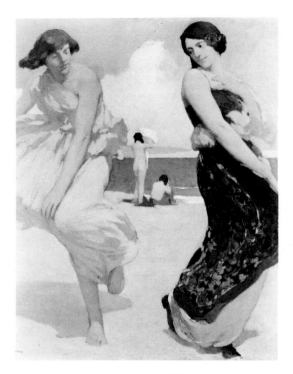

(cat. no. 42)
Arthur F. Mathews
Dancing Girls on Carmel Beach

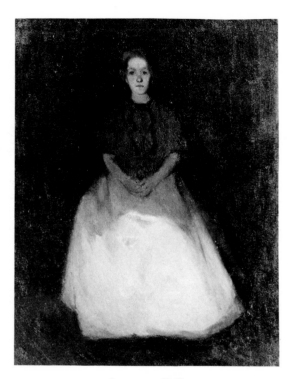

(cat. no. 102)
Lucia K. Mathews
Red and White

FURTHER regional aspects of this so-called style derive from the Mathews' followers. Although there was never a movement or a school of art *per se* that could be identified with Mathews in the way certain other art movements were created, evidence of his widespread influence among California artists is evident. As a teacher at the Mark Hopkins Institute of Art he did not encourage students to paint in his style. He insisted that they should find their own way. Mathews said, "A great artist succeeds because he is different . . . of course artists are born but they must discipline their ability."

Despite his intentions, Mathews was a strong influence upon the artistic style of many of his students and associates. Certain aspects of the California Decorative style can be seen in the works of several noted California artists. Gottardo Piazzoni, Xavier Martinez, Francis McComas, Carl Armin Hansen and of course Lucia Mathews are but a few artists whose works bear testimony to the master's influence. Interestingly, it was in the landscape tradition that Mathews' style was carried on. There is little evidence of their continuation of his interest in the great allegories from the murals and easel paintings or in the familiar dancing figures. These were truly his unique expressions within the style.

Murals

THE most exacting and complicated form of painting is the art of the muralist. It encompasses a broad range of disciplines relative to painting and architecture and demands considerable experience and self-assurance of an artist. The World's Columbian Exposition of 1893 in Chicago provided the impetus for a reawakened interest in mural painting among American artists. Prior to that event, mural painting was practiced chiefly by European artists.

Arthur Mathews was by this time already an admirer of the great French muralist Puvis de Chavannes, from whose works he had absorbed the salient concepts of the form. It was as California's finest muralist that Mathews was known during his lifetime and since. National recognition of his achievements in this specialized art form came in 1923, when the American Institute of Architects awarded him its Fine Arts Gold Medal.

Mathews received his first mural commission in 1896 for the decorations in the library of the Horace L. Hill mansion in San Francisco. He devised an "endless" frieze, three feet high and one hundred eight feet long, which was continuous along the four walls next to the ceiling. The panorama depicted *The Arts of Peace* (cat. no. 81). Various subjects of the frieze included *Music and the Dance, Romance and Poesy,* and *The Industries,* and all were represented by groups of figures in a landscape setting. The classical style of the mural, reminiscent of Puvis de Chavannes, was planned to be in harmony with the Grecian-inspired furnishings of the room. Mathews reportedly had canvas specially made which would absorb the oil paint and provide a non-reflective surface for the mural. The painting was executed in Mathews' studio, then the finished mural was pasted on the wall. This was the technique he used on all his subsequent murals.

Several commissions for decorations of this type came during the next few years. Mathews painted two large round ceiling panels depicting Cupid and Psyche, and Spring for the drawing room of the home of F. M. Smith (the Borax magnate) in Oakland. Arthur's brother, Walter P. Mathews, was the architect of the Smith mansion.

Seven panels with designs based upon pastoral themes were created for the home of W. A. Dingee in San Francisco. Later, Mathews completed several panels in comparable motifs for the residence of R. J. Taussig, then president of the Mechanics Institute. Mathews painted two murals for the vestibule of the Mechanics Institute Library; the first mural was part of a complete decoration which was destroyed by the 1906 earthquake and fire, and the second one is a replacement for the original.

Upon completion of a new Carnegie library building for Oakland in 1902, Arthur Mathews was commissioned to design a series of murals for the two large rooms on the second floor. The original plan called for twelve large panels, of which only six were eventually completed. The first two murals were displayed at the Mark Hopkins Institute before their installation in Oakland in 1904. The theme of the first panel was *Nature* (cat. no. 82), symbolically depicted as mother and child.

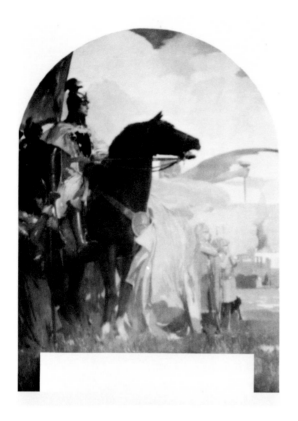

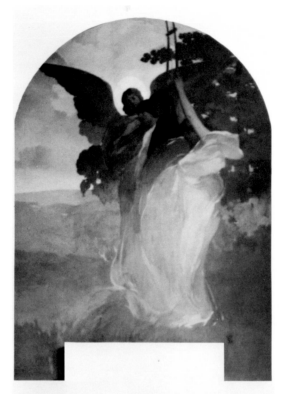

(cat. no. 85)
Arthur F. Mathews
Conquest, 1907

(cat. no. 84)
Arthur F. Mathews
Resignation, 1907

Its companion panel titled *The Arts* (cat. no. 83) shows two women decorating a vase. Typical Mathews features of these murals are the female figures in decorative "Grecian" gowns, the obviously California landscape and his favorite "Art and Nature" theme. The second set of two completed panels was destroyed during the 1906 disaster while still in Mathews' studio. The replacement murals were installed in the library less than a year after the fire. The first of the new set of panels was called *Conquest* (cat. no. 85) and depicted a European knight on horseback in quest of glory in California. Its companion piece, titled *Resignation* (cat. no. 84), presented a contrasting theme intended to represent peace and harmony. Only *The Soil* and *The Grain,* the first two of four murals planned for the *Wheat Series,* were actually completed. By 1908, when those two California landscapes were placed on the library walls, the mural funds had been depleted and no additional moneys were appropriated to finish the project as originally proposed.

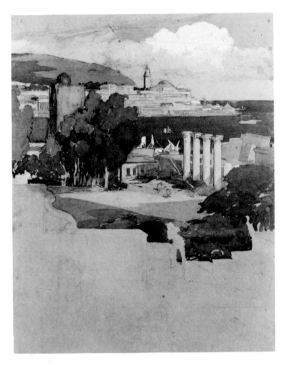

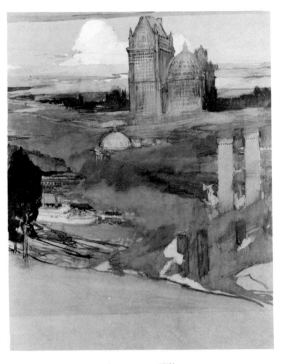

(cat. no. 74)
Arthur F. Mathews
Sketch for "The City", 1913

(cat. no. 77)
Arthur F. Mathews
Sketch for "Modern City", 1913

The most imposing example of Mathews' mural art can be seen in the state capitol rotunda at Sacramento. The series of twelve panels, completed and installed in 1914, traces the epic development of life in California. Four groups of three panels each deal with a different epoch in the history of California. Under the titles: *Adventure, The Mission Era, The Pioneers,* and *The City,* Mathews depicted scenes of the Indians, the explorers, the missionaries, the settlers, the gold rush, the development of industry and the arts, and finally, his impression of a city of the future. In order to best serve the decorative function of these murals, Mathews chose to portray the romance and gran-

deur of his subjects instead of the realism and drama. Technically, he executed these murals in the idiom of his characteristic California Decorative Style, but they are not as well unified with their architectural setting as his other large murals.

Arthur Mathews was deeply involved in several aspects of the 1915 Panama-Pacific International Exposition. In addition to his active interest in the plans for the event, and his participation as a judge and an exhibitor, his most notable contribution was a mural titled, *The Victorious Spirit* (illus. page 28). Mathews was the only Californian among a distinguished group of artists selected to create mural decorations for the exhibition buildings. Located

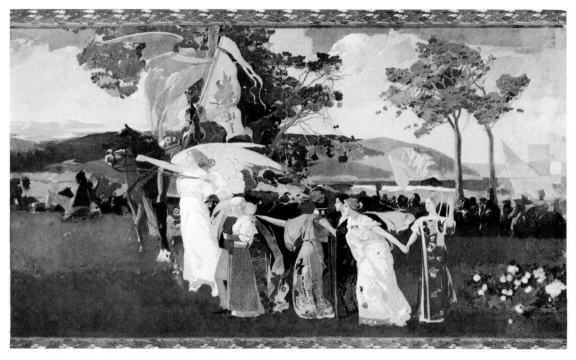

(cat. no. 86)
Arthur F. Mathews
Untitled mural

in the lunette shaped space over the main doorway of "The Court of Palms," his allegorical painting showed a golden winged "angel of light" protecting a youth and his guardians from a brutal equestrian figure representing the "spirit of materialism." His mural was thought to be one of the very best created for the occasion.

In the years following the exposition, Mathews continued to be the dominant muralist of the region. His major commissions included murals for the library of The Mechanics Institute, (a replacement for the one destroyed in the 1906 fire), panels for the Columbia and Curran Theaters, *The Commonwealth* (cat. no. 88) for the Supreme Court chamber of the State Building in San Francisco and two panels

for "The Catacombs" of Cypress Lawn Cemetery (cat. no. 87). Mathews' last important commission was in 1934 for decorations and murals in the lobby of the St. Francis Hotel.

Aside from his murals, Mathews produced two other outstanding architecturally oriented decorations: the design of four relief panels for the pair of massive bronze doors on the Savings Union Bank (1911), and his splendid design in stained glass for the Franc Pierce Hammon memorial window (cat. no. 89) for the San Francisco Women's City Club (1925). In both cases, Mathews closely supervised other craftsmen in the execution of his original designs, but did not work directly with bronze or glass in his own studio.

Paintings

IN 1885, when Arthur Mathews was a young man of twenty-five about to begin studies at the Académie Julian in Paris, he was already an artist of some professional experience. His architectural training in his father's office and the practice he acquired as a designer and illustrator for Britton and Rey Lithographers in San Francisco demonstrated his technical proficiency as a draftsman. However, little of what Mathews produced in those early years seemed to anticipate the high degree of originality and technical facility that marked his mature work. An interest in the human figure is indicated in most of his drawings and designs that date from 1879 to 1885. Even his architectural designs for a building interior and the proposal for the Washington Monument included figures in the murals, ornamentation and statuary. The successful accomplishments of his youth notwithstanding, Mathews recognized the need for training of a type not then available in San Francisco. Only Paris offered the kind of preparation Mathews thought was necessary to the artist he aspired to be. Paris provided exposure to the great art of the past and the opportunity to participate in the vitality of all the arts during that period.

Mathews was prepared both by disposition and experience to accept the emphasis placed upon a sound technique and a figurative style which were characteristic of the French art academies. At the Académie Julian, he was quick to learn the lessons of the masters Boulanger and Lefebvre, whose credentials represented

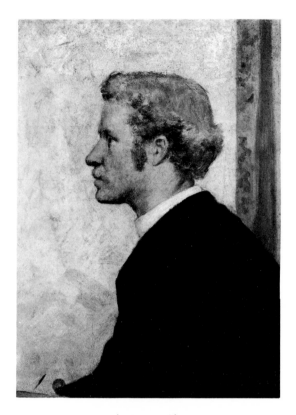

(cat. no. 2)
Arthur F. Mathews
Portrait of a Young Gentleman, 1886

the official academic point of view. Mathews soon became known as the best draftsman of all the American students at the Academy. His superior performance in each of the three major disciplines — drawing, painting, and composition — earned for him the coveted Grand Gold Medal of the Académie Julian. Arthur Mathews' paintings from those student years quite naturally reflect the artistic taste and criteria associated with the so-called "academic style."

His first paintings accepted in the Paris Salon (1887) were the *Portrait of a Young Gentleman* and *Imogen and Aviragus.* Both

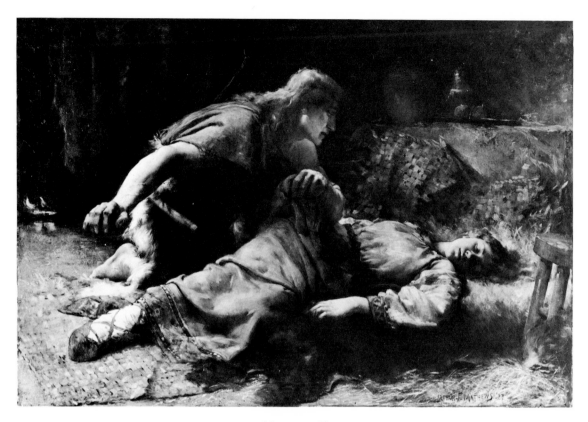

(Cat. no. 3)
Arthur F. Mathews
Imogen and Arviragus, 1887

works attest to his high level of technical achievement in adherence to the academic criteria. In *Portrait of a Young Gentleman* (cat. no. 2), Mathews displayed competence in portraiture with a sensitive profile study that showed particularly skillful color effects in his rendering of the flesh tints. A faint inscription in the upper left corner of the painting indicates the portrait is probably of Mathews' artist friend, Edward Willis Redfield, then a student in Paris. In *Imogen and Arviragus* (cat. no. 3), Mathews demonstrated his ability to develop a painting from literary material, an approach characteristic of "official" painters of the academies. The painting took its subject from Shakespeare's *Cymbeline* and shows Imogen asleep in the cave. The painting may be seen as an exercise dealing with various academic problems. The presentation of figures in difficult positions, the illusion of three dimensional forms in a logical space and a rendering of the details of color and textures are successfully accomplished along with the projection of warm human sentiment.

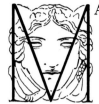ATHEW'S earliest painting which offers an indication of what was to come in his mature style is *The Lilies of Midas* (cat. no. 7), exhibited in the Paris Salon in 1889. Its subject, somewhat prophetic for his use of a theme from Greek mythology, depicts an incident from the story of King Midas. The greedy king's "gift" of "the golden touch" is suggested by his upturned hands and by the intense golden light that suffuses the scene. Here was Mathews' first use of an overall dominant color tonality with which he was able both to unify the various elements of the painting and to convey the theme and mood of the work.

The next development toward Mathews' mature style of painting was a move away from the strict realism of his student works. Following his return to San Francisco in 1889, his paintings placed greater emphasis upon formal considerations. A simplification of forms executed in flat color areas replaced his former preoccupation with pictorial details.

During a period of technical experimentation, Mathews toyed with certain Impressionist ideas related to depicting lighting effects through color. In 1893, he produced over a hundred and thirty sketches out of doors, in pastels and oils, in preparation for his large painting *A Picnic at El Campo*. The many studies of light upon landscape settings and on figures, both singly and in groups, suggested the scientific approach of the French Impressionists. The ultimate product of Mathews' efforts was an ambitious composition that depicted more than fifty figures skillfully arranged in a way that avoided a crowded

appearance. The only evidence that remains of Mathews' brief, albeit tentative, foray into Impressionist territory is a photograph (illus. page 20) and a single figure sketch, *Woman in a Park* (cat. no. 13), done in colors almost more Tonalist than Impressionist.

The 1894 Midwinter Fair provided the first showing of French Impressionist paintings in San Francisco. Mathews' own less-than-enthusiastic response to that exhibition may have caused him to abandon further use of Impressionist methods or techniques in his later works. He disliked Impressionist color which he found to be without proper harmony. He felt Impressionism was too much concerned with factual material and that it was too literal and lacked a subjective interpretation "necessary" to a work of art.

Mathews' particular aesthetic sensibility was more attracted to a decorative approach to painting like that of Whistler. His use of a subdued color tonality and the flat, generalized forms executed in a loose painterly technique appealed to Mathews' insistence upon a personal interpretation. There was an increased emphasis upon formal "design" considerations manifest in a number of his paintings from the mid-1890's. His organically conceived compositions stressed flat patterns of interlocking shapes and sweeping, rhythmic lines.

A brief thematic explication or form analysis of a few of Arthur Mathews' paintings is useful to discern a philosophical consistency throughout his work; further, it should provide some insight into the significance of various paintings not here discussed in detail.

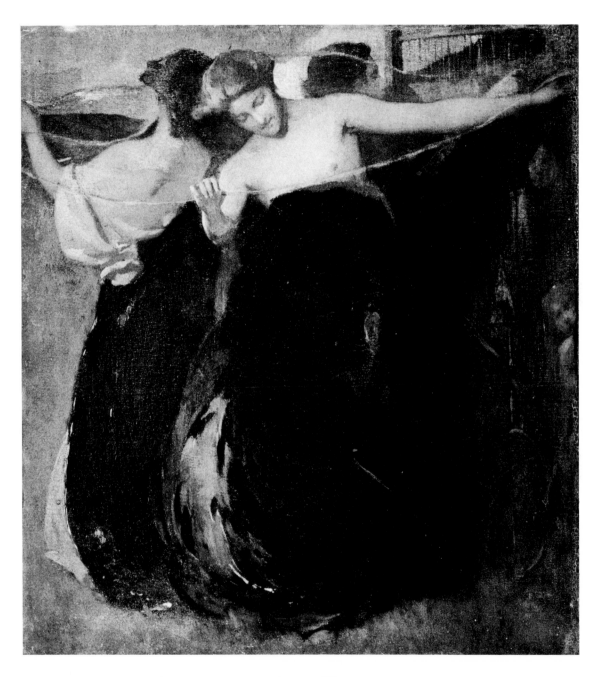

(cat. no. 10)
Arthur F. Mathews
The Web (The Three Fates)

SUBJECTS that Mathews chose to portray came frequently from Biblical and mythical sources. Evidence that remains of such works as *Judith, Hagar and Ishmael, The Death of Abel* and *Adam and Eve* (all presumed lost) suggests a mystical interpretation that is quite different from nineteenth century piety or religiosity. His painting of *Eve* (cat. no. 8) is characteristic of the aforementioned group. A Symbolist influence is suggested by the inexplicable radiant apparition which appears behind the nude figure of Eve. An overt theatricality which dominates this and other of his Biblical paintings was abandoned in the later works. The stylistic precedent for *Eve* may be seen as a synthesis of various decorative elements to be found in the disparate styles of Whistler and Gauguin. That the concept of overall subdued color tonality owes much to Whistler is understood, and Gauguin's influence does not seem so far-fetched if one considers the forms independent of his characteristic color. Perhaps the best example of Gauguin's influence upon Mathews' painting style can be seen in *The Grape* (cat. no. 26). Even in the color, although more subdued than Gauguin's, there is some suggestion of his decorative approach. The vast difference in temperament between the two artists precludes philosophical parallels in their works. Although some of Mathews' subject matter was potentially erotic or emotional, he chose to present it with a cool detachment that clearly avoids identification with the passionate temperament of Gauguin. Mathews insisted upon a delicate balance of the objective and the subjective aspects in a painting. It was no doubt owing to

that particular classical bias that Mathews avoided the attraction to a somewhat more stylized or abstracted approach to painting as practiced by the Post-Impressionists and *Les Nabis*. Mathews said that they had overdone their emphasis on form and although his own paintings were perfect in design, he "didn't throw it at you."

Consistent with his classical orientation were the subjects he chose to portray. Mathews frequently took themes from Greek and Roman antiquity which were common to sculpture, architecture and vase painting, and therefore appropriate to his decorative applications.

The Grecian philosophy which equated art and nature became a favorite theme in many Mathews paintings and murals. His painting titled *Art and Nature* (cat. no. 21) metaphorically depicts the concept in figurative terms. However, it is not absolutely clear whether he subscribed to the classical Greek notion which identified art with the perfection of the nude figure or whether to the nineteenth-century tendency to reverse the symbolism and identify the nude with nature. In many of Mathews' allegorical paintings and murals the attributes of "art" are represented by the decorative garments which adorned the female figures. The ambiguity of these symbols is further complicated by his version of *Sacred and Profane Love* (cat. no. 32). His original title for the painting was *The Carnation* which must have been even more confusing to anyone unfamiliar with the archaic meaning of the word, which referred to the carnal. The theme and composition of Mathews' painting bears a resemblance to Titian's *Sacred and Profane Love*, but there is a strong indication that the symbolism of the nude and the clothed figures have been reversed

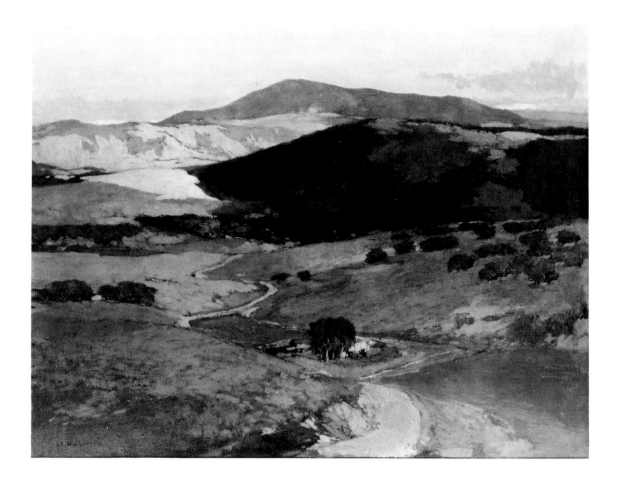

(cat. no. 33)
Arthur F. Mathews
View From Skyline Boulevard

from Titian's Neo-Platonic iconography. In Mathews' version, the clothed figure holding the winged attribute of victory implies the sacred spirit, while the nude modestly presenting her back to the observer can be seen playing the pipes of Pan. Pan in mythology is usually identified with the earthly and playful pursuits —hence "profane" from a Victorian standpoint.

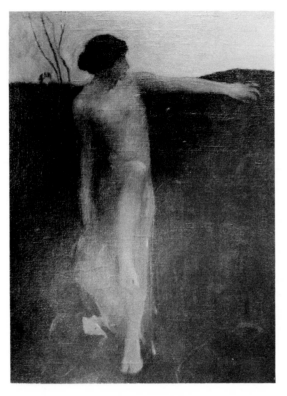

(Cat. no. 9)
Arthur F. Mathews
The Butterfly
Collection of The Oakland Museum

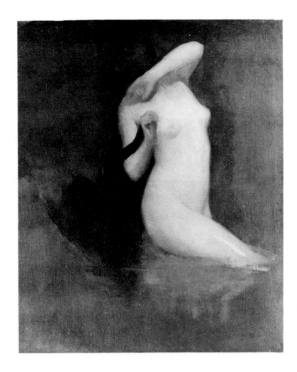

(cat. no. 20)
Arthur F. Mathews
The Swan
Collection of The Oakland Museum

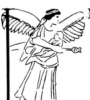N the paintings titled *The Swan, the Butterfly,* and *The Wave,* he further reveals his Greek sources in depicting themes from nature metaphorically represented by the human figure. *The Swan* (cat. no. 20) is appropriately depicted as a graceful feminine figure bathing in a pool. The black robe falling from her shoulders is draped in a way which subtly suggests the arched neck of a swan. The resultant imagery may call to mind *Leda and the Swan.*

His painting *The Butterfly* (cat. no. 9) reveals a dual representation of the theme. Metaphorically the dancing figure seems to suggest the imminent flight of the butterfly that appears on her outstretched hand. Perhaps the painting, with its misty atmosphere and low-keyed color tonality reminiscent of Whistler, was intended as a subtle tribute to this great master whose monogram was a butterfly. Mathews himself indulged in a similar conceit when he signed a few illustrations with a monogram of a bee fashioned from his own initials.

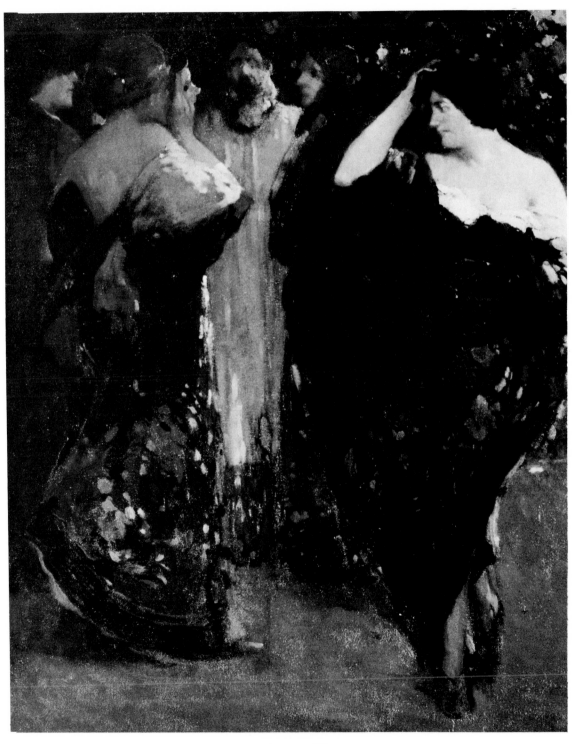

(cat. no. 34)
Arthur F. Mathews
A Masque

62

THETIS, the mythological sea nymph who could change her shape to become anything she desired, was possibly Mathews' thematic source of *The Wave* (cat. no. 23). According to the myth, in one of Thetis' transformations she became an ocean wave. Formalistically, Mathews' organic arrangement of curvilinear forms in *The Wave* came closer to a popular concept of *L'Art Nouveau* manner in painting than any of his other works. Mathews' interest in the peacock image was one he shared with *L'Art Nouveau*. Although he seldom made use of its potential for the pure design effects that fascinated artists such as Beardsley or Tiffany, he was attracted to its symbolism. A case in point is Mathews' *The Mandarin Robe* (cat. no. 22), which explores a dual symbolism of the peacock which he used in many paintings and murals: its intrinsically decorative or aesthetic connotation and also its traditional symbolism for vanity. A humorous parallel is drawn here in the way the figure, clad in the splendid decorative robe, regards the exotic bird at her side.

This extension of themes from nature to include "human nature" resulted in his use of some rather complex symbolism in *The Masque of Pandora* and *I Piped but Ye Would Not Dance*. Mathews was apparently fascinated by the Pandora myth because he repeated it in other paintings and illustrations. In Greek mythology, Pandora was the first woman on earth. Because of her curiosity she is held responsible for releasing all the evils of the world from the jar or box in which they were kept. Mathews' first *Pandora* (now pre-

sumed lost) was exhibited in the Paris Exposition Universelle in 1889. His 1914-15 version titled *The Masque of Pandora* (cat. no. 31) alludes to the definition of "masque" as an ancient theatrical presentation based upon mythical or allegorical themes. Mathews has placed Pandora to the right of three other figures that apparently represent the Fates: Spinner, Portioner and Never-turn-back. That his symbolism is subject to various interpretations remains consistent with Symbolist inclinations. The absence of a clear or absolute symbolism in art was precisely what appealed to the Symbolists in Europe. However, the frame with its Egyptian motifs was not actually intended for that particular painting and should not be confused with its symbolism.

Another allegory of art is the apparent subject of *I Piped But Ye Would Not Dance* (cat. no. 35). An altered version of a quote from the New Testament: Matthew XI, 17, "We have piped unto you and ye have not danced," it also seems to carry a different meaning. An oversimplified interpretation of the Biblical meaning may be read as the Pharisees rejecting the gospel of Jesus and John. In Mathews' painting, the meaning is more likely to follow that of a sculpture by Gutzon Borglum which bears the same title. Borglum had explained his sculpture to Mathews in this way: "the saddest thing in life is that the best given us is neglected or suffered to pass, its true value being discovered only when gone out of reach or hearing." In Mathews' own somewhat didactic version, he suggests that the arts, typically represented by the female figure in a peacock gown, are rejected by some kind of uncultured force, here represented as a sword-carrying male

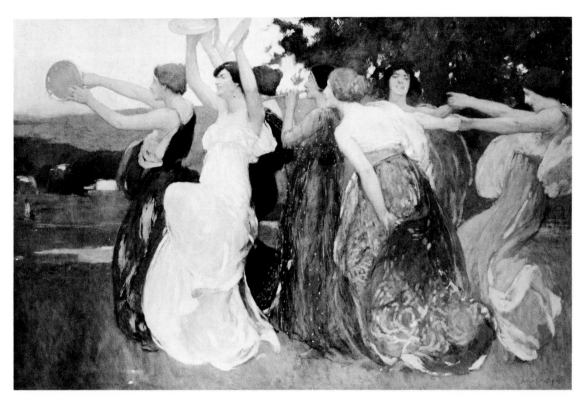

(cat. no. 39)
Arthur F. Mathews
Dancing Figures, 1917

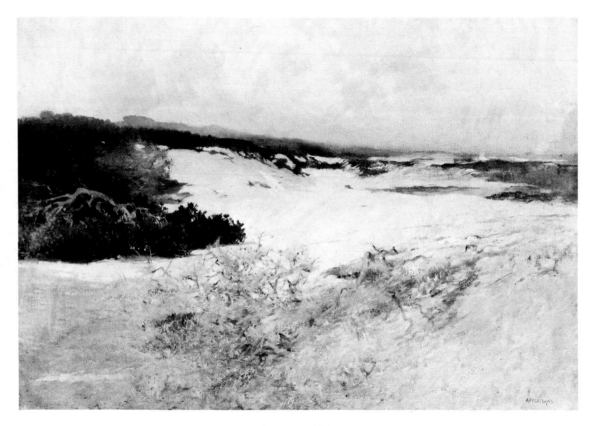

(cat. no. 28)
Arthur F. Mathews
Monterey Beach

figure. (The painting with its California setting could be interpreted as Mathews' cynical assessment of the local art scene.) In addition to a further allusion to the allegories of art and nature, this painting shows his typical dualism of concepts and the symmetrical orientation of his themes.

Mathews' landscape paintings were apparently unencumbered by the symbolism that accompanied his figurative works. He took great pleasure in depicting the hills and trees of coastal California with their characteristic forms, colors and surrounding atmosphere. Nature was his constant source of inspiration and his best teacher. He had the remarkable ability to capture the essential qualities of the California scenery with simple direct means. Most of his landscapes were products of visits to the Monterey peninsula and as such bear that unmistakable identity. As would be expected, the landscapes adhere to the decorative criteria of his other works.

When he combined the classic allegorical figures with his California panoramas the result was uniquely "Mathews." Two paintings which can be seen as the culmination of his California Decorative style are *California* and *Youth.*

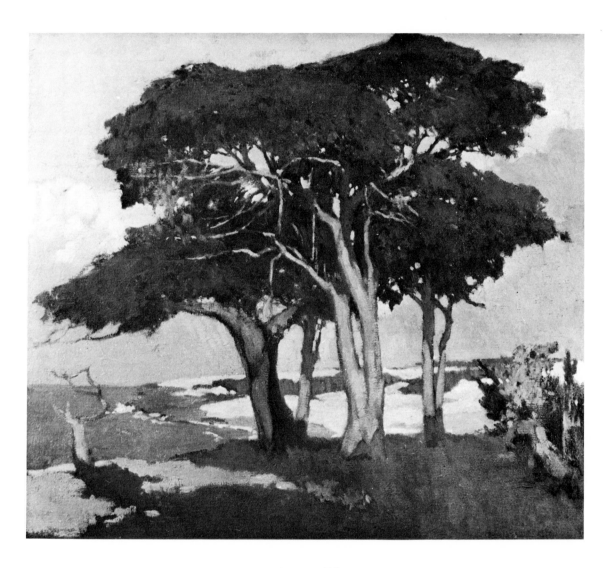

(cat. no. 54)
Arthur F. Mathews
Monterey Cypress #1

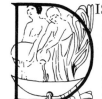**D**ISTINCTIVE features of the style in both works are the heavy ornamental frames Mathews designed for these particular paintings. The requisite harmony between frame and painting seems less strained if one considers the common theme and decorative function of both components.

In *California* (cat. no. 27) Mathews brings together both pictorial and symbolical material to represent his subject. The background landscape and sea beyond have been thematically reinforced by certain subtle references to California in the frame design, i.e., California poppies, oak leaves, etc. The implantation of culture in his home state, a favorite Mathews theme, is here symbolized by the two Grecian-inspired figures and the book. The book, indicative of cultivation through higher learning, is laid open before a personification of California.

The painting of festive dancing figures titled *Youth* (cat. no. 38) is perhaps the keystone of the Mathews *oeuvre*. This work encompasses virtually all of the individual elements of his mature style: a muralist's flat decorative approach, compositional devices inspired by Japanese prints, subdued color tonality and his organically conceived rhythms of line and pattern. Thematically it is consistent for its presentation of allegories of art and nature in California. Here the nine dancing women in the foreground suggest the muses from classic mythology while they portray the spirit of youth with their frolic in music and dance. The astrological symbols which decorate the skirt of one dancer conveys a contemporary significance to "youth" that was doubtfully intentional. Of particular interest is the archaic musical instrument depicted in this painting, and repeated in several of Mathews' other works, identified as an aulos. Like so many of his thematic sources, it is Greek in origin. This double pipe "flute" was the prototype of some modern wind instruments. The peculiar strap or band shown stretched across the mouth of the musician is called a phorbeia and was used to support the player's inflated cheeks. The strongest thematic element of the painting is revealed in the characteristic regional landscape which completes Mathews' visual paean to youth and the arts in California.

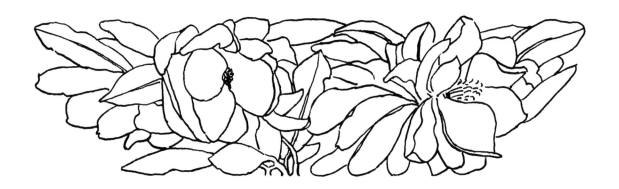

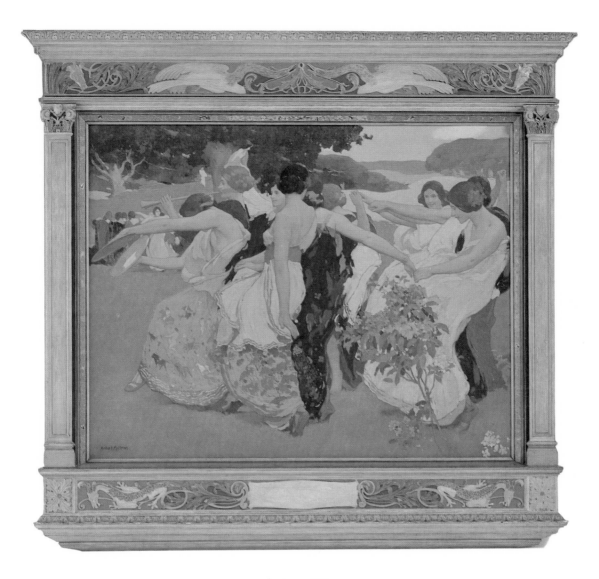

(cat. no. 38)
Arthur F. Mathews
Youth

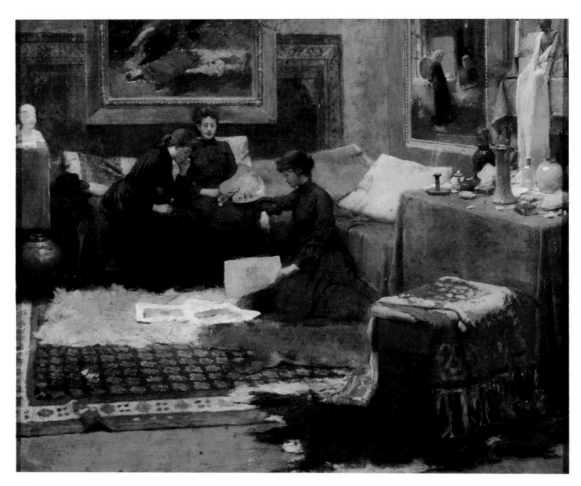

(cat. no. 5)
Arthur F. Mathews
Paris Studio Interior

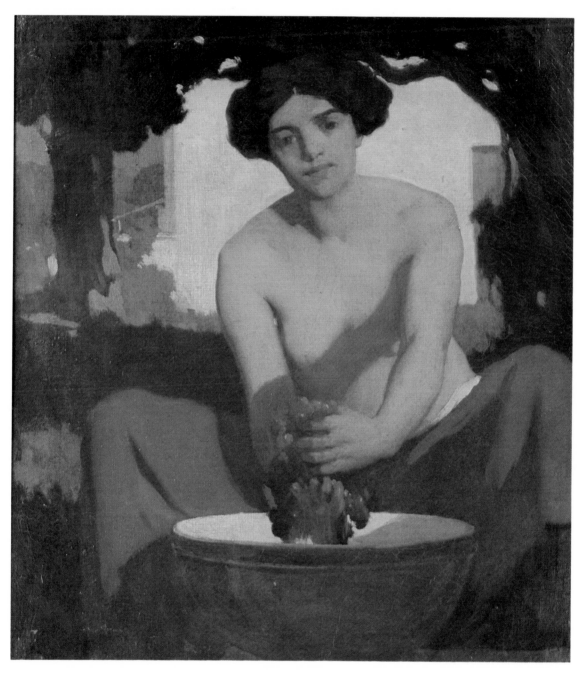

(cat. no. 26)
Arthur F. Mathews
The Grape

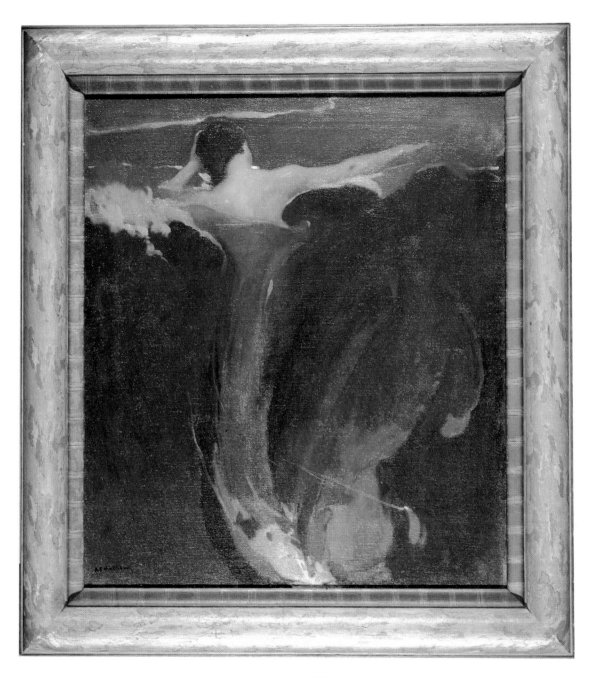

(cat. no. 23)
Arthur F. Mathews
The Wave

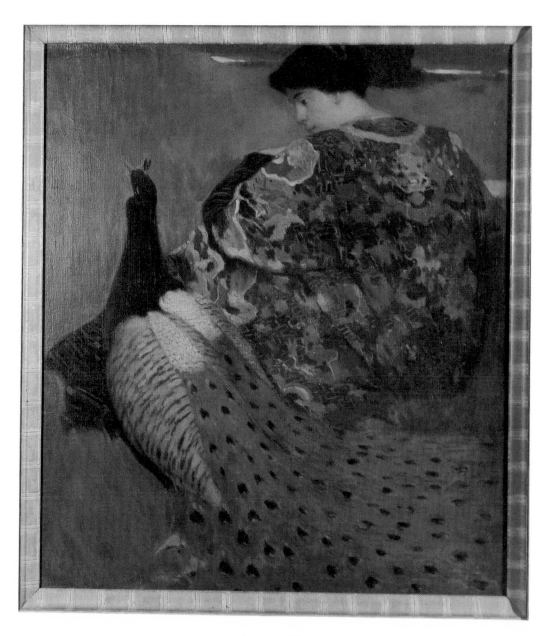

(cat. no. 22)
Arthur F. Mathews
Mandarin Robe

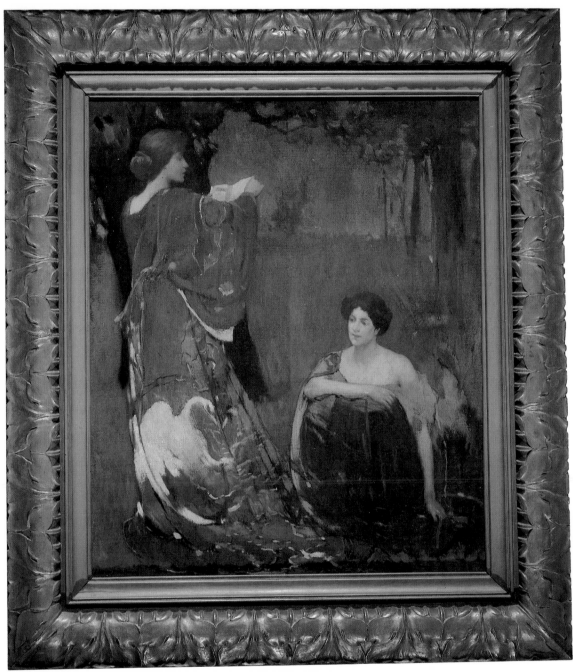

(cat. no. 11)
Arthur F. Mathews
Two Figures

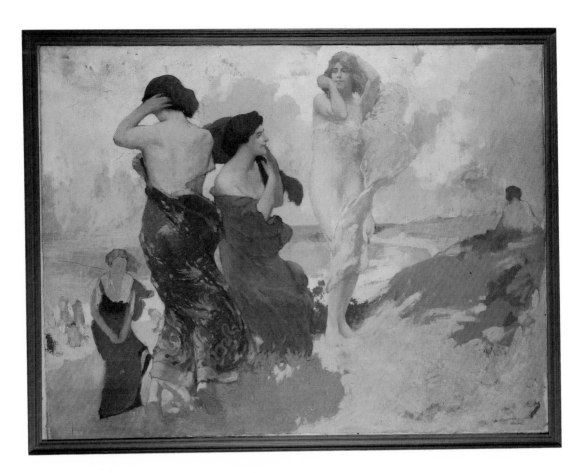

(cat. no. 37)
Arthur F. Mathews
Dancing Girls

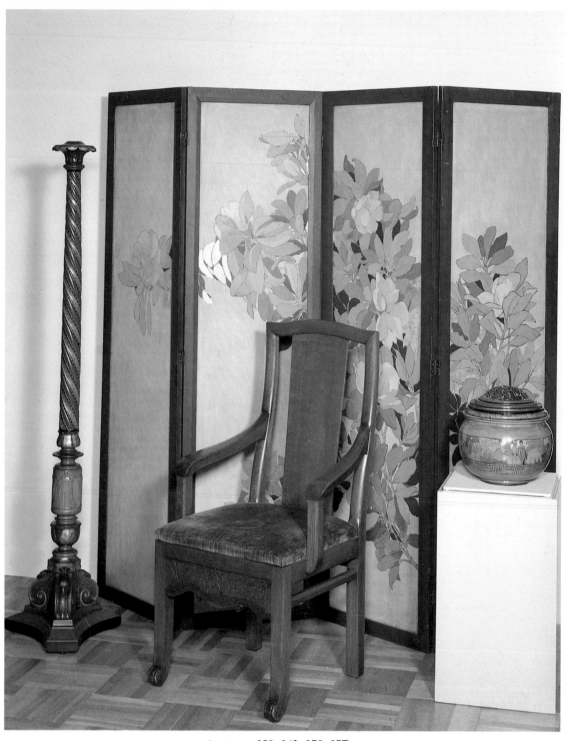

(cat. nos. 139, 142, 156, 157)
Objects by Furniture Shop

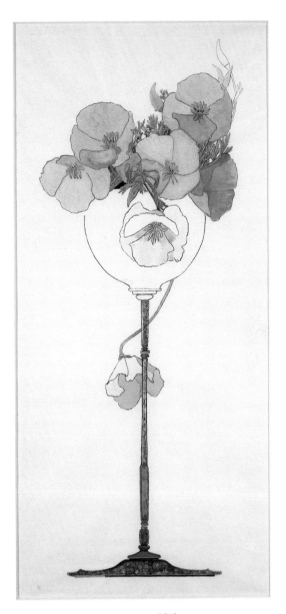

(cat. no. 134)
Lucia K. Mathews
California Poppies in Tall Goblet

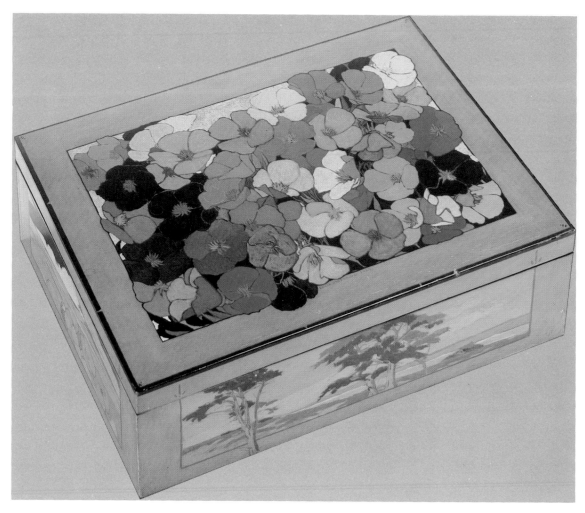

(cat. no. 145)
Lucia K. Mathews
Box with Lid, 1929

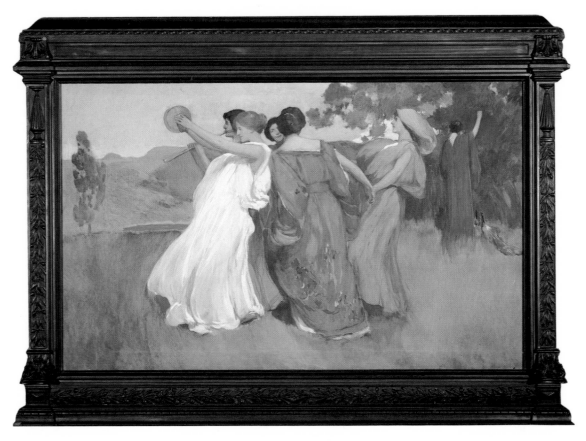

Arthur F. Mathews
Dancing Girls #4

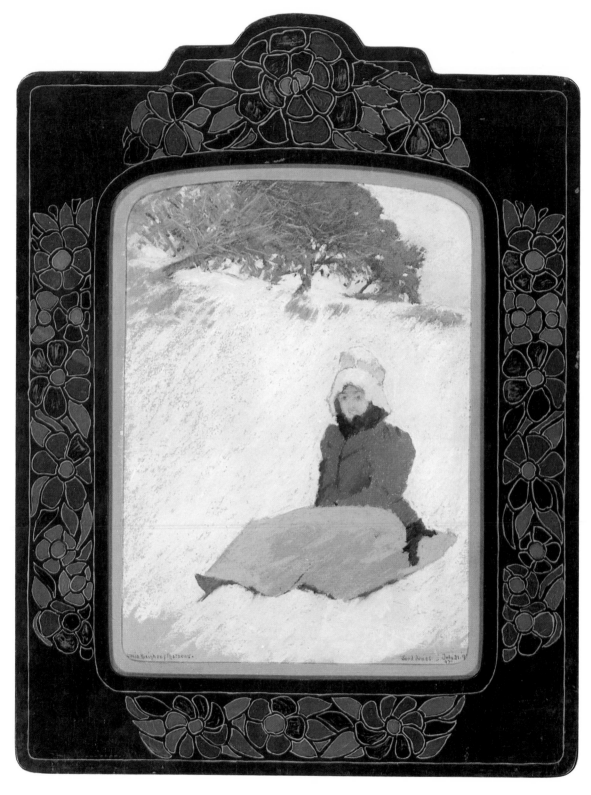

(cat. no. 113)
Lucia K. Mathews
Seated Girl on Sand Dunes

Paintings by Lucia K. Mathews

THE emphasis placed on a discussion of the paintings by Arthur Mathews serves mainly to define the style, and does by no means intend any implication of superior quality over Lucia's works. That Lucia's paintings and decorative objects fit within the definition of the California Decorative style is evident, and that her works show the influence of Arthur is perhaps obvious, but there remains that special accent within the style that is uniquely hers. Arthur Mathews himself had said, on more than one occasion, that Lucia might have been the greater artist. Her best efforts, although fewer in number and smaller in scale, attest to the notion that she was at least his equal in most respects.

She began her formal art training at the Mark Hopkins Institute, where Arthur, as the teacher, recognized her remarkable talent. She eventually became his private pupil and then his wife.

Her student works are highly competent examples of typical academic exercises, but some of her more mature works suggest a working style somewhat advanced of Arthur's by modern standards. Her pastels and oil sketches of figures on the beach from the late 1890's are reminiscent of Boudin or Vuillard and Denis.

During a visit to Europe with Arthur and their friend Louise Schwamm in 1898-99, Lucia took the opportunity to study briefly with Whistler at his Académie Carmen in Paris. His influence upon her painting at that time can be seen in her palette as well as in the subject matter. A tiny oil sketch of the *River Seine* (cat. no. 94) is a typically Whistlerian nocturne executed with a sensitivity and expression of mood worthy of the master.

Despite her obvious success with that style, Lucia later turned from Whistler's influence to develop her own personal stylistic identity.

Scale is a significant factor in distinguishing between Arthur and Lucia's individual painting styles. Unlike her husband, she did not approach painting from an architect's or a muralist's orientation. Although Lucia Mathews clearly understood the modernist principles which relate pictorial imagery to a flat surface, she employed them to a different effect. Hers was a somewhat more "painterly" technique than Arthur's. The relatively small size of her oil paintings allowed for a more direct means of description that utilized the quality of brush-stroke to better advantage. As a result her paintings project an intimacy with an immediate appeal sometimes lacking in Arthur's grandiose creations.

A preference for the watercolor technique resulted in virtual abandonment of oils in the early 1900's. She combined her interest in gardening with that of painting with watercolors to produce a large number of floral paintings over the years. This particular interest was further manifest in the floral decorations on furniture and various tabletop objects produced at the Furniture Shop. Her imagery was more direct and simple, even when it included the figure, than Arthur's complicated allegories. Despite certain common characteristics in their paintings — figures, California landscape, and emphasis on a

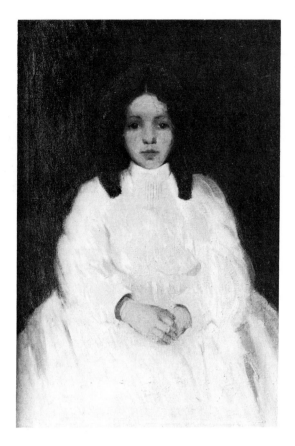

(cat. no. 104)
Lucia K. Mathews
Child in White

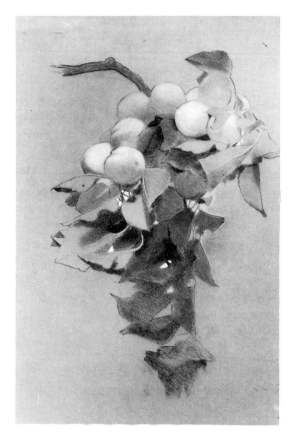

(cat. no. 118)
Lucia K. Mathews
Apricots #3, 1908

decorativeness — Lucia's works are distinctive.

Her separate identity in the California Decorative style is well demonstrated by her watercolor *Portrait of Red-Haired Girl* (cat. no. 123). The sensitive portrait of the little girl under the orange tree is surrounded by the frame bearing an orange motif carved in low relief and painted in perfect harmony with the watercolor.

The frequent trips to the Monterey region resulted in a large number of watercolor landscapes in which she depicted the same cypress, pine and oak trees along green and gold hillsides that Arthur painted in oils. One of these watercolors won for her a silver medal at the Panama-Pacific International Exposition in 1915. The floral designs or vignettes that decorated the pages of *Philopolis* magazine and many books from Philopolis Press were often Lucia's creations.

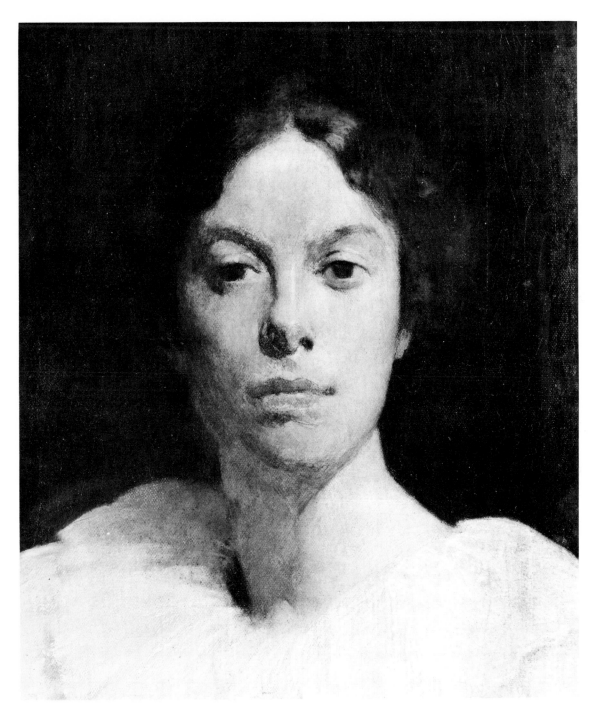

(cat. no. 17)
Arthur F. Mathews
Portrait of Lucia Mathews

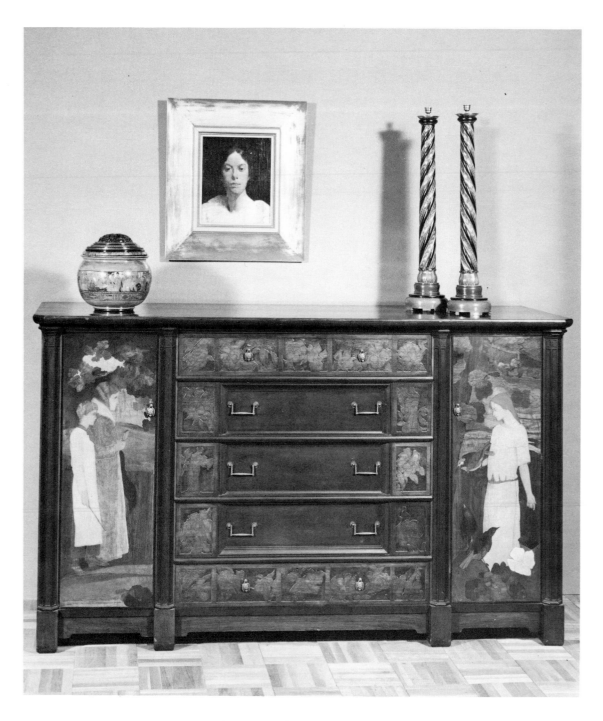

(cat. nos. 157, 17, 149, 158)
Objects by Furniture Shop,
Arthur F. and Lucia K. Mathews

HE great fire of 1906 can be seen as a pivotal point in the multiplex art careers of Arthur and Lucia Mathews. For him it marked a turning away from teaching that freed him to direct his prodigious talents toward more diversified activities and interests. For her it began a period of increased opportunities to make use of her special artistic abilities and to collaborate in many of Arthur's projects. This was the beginning of a twenty-year period that produced most of their best known works and is most characteristic of their California Decorative Style.

The focus of this burst of activity was the Furniture Shop—a humble name for the grand enterprise it was to house. This result of a highly fortunate business partnership between Arthur Mathews and John Zeile, his good friend and a devoted patron of art, was to last until 1920. Here was the Mathews base of operation that included projects in architecture, interior decoration, furniture design and construction, wood crafts, city planning, writing and publications.

Arthur Mathews himself designed the brown shingled Furniture Shop structure. It was conceived in the Craftsman Style with additional characteristic traces of Oriental influence. The building had a certain stylistic resemblance to the works of his contemporary, architect Bernard May-beck. This was the first building built after the fire to house artists' studios; William Keith and Arthur Mathews both had studios on the second floor. During the first year in the building, the Furniture Shop shared space with the Beach-Robinson Furniture Company. John Zeile was also a partner in that company and until its relocation in 1907 it maintained a showroom at the front of the building.

During that period of intense rebuilding activity in San Francisco, the Furniture Shop was kept busy trying to meet a demand for high quality custom-designed home furnishings and decoration. In the partnership John Zeile functioned as business manager while Arthur Mathews was the master designer. Lucia supervised much of the carving and attended to details of design and color. She did many of the small objects herself that required carved or painted decoration. Designers, cabinet makers, wood carvers and other craftsmen that numbered from twenty to as many as fifty for some of the larger projects, were employed by the Furniture Shop. Arthur's assistant designer, Thomas McGlynn, was his former student from the School of Design. As Mathews' chief assistant, McGlynn was responsible for many details in the execution of the master's designs.

The shop received commissions from private individuals as well as in sub-contract to architectural firms.

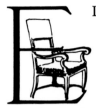**E**LEGANT custom interiors were created, complete to the smallest detail, with Furniture Shop products and designs. Decorations included wood paneling, murals, easel paintings with custom frames, all the furniture, specially designed fixtures, and accessories. Everything was conceived by Mathews to be in perfect harmony, a concept that brings to mind Whistler's famous Peacock Room. The practices of the Furniture Shop were clearly consonant with the widespread concept of the elevation of applied arts, and the merging of the arts in general, that was so basic to the Arts and Crafts Movement — all of which suggests William Morris in its scope and its social aspects, However, despite certain similarities, there is little evidence beyond a superficial comparison to indicate any direct relationship either philosophically or stylistically, between Morris and Mathews. The rather general influence of the English Arts and Crafts Movement on American artists can be acknowledged, for Mathews was fully aware of such developments. One elemental difference lies in their individual conceptual bias. Morris took inspiration from Medieval Europe while Mathews harkened to Classical antiquity —contradictions in both style and ethic. Another comparison is suggested between the Furniture Shop and the Roycrofters of East Aurora, New York, which was its contemporary. William Morris' devoted follower in this country, Elbert Hubbard, headed an operation that had similarities to the Mathews' enterprise, i.e., furniture, crafts, and publications, among others. But it was conceived along considerably more socialistic and moralistic lines.

The products of the Furniture Shop can be separated into two categories: those works which belong to large suites of matching pieces designed to meet the requirements of various clients; and those which are truly unique, the fantastic personalized pieces that Arthur and Lucia seemed to keep for themselves and their friends. Quite naturally the former category exists in greater quantity and is less distinctive. This does not qualify its relation to other custom or mass-produced furniture, because every Mathews-designed piece had its own character.

The most ambitious undertaking of ensemble works by the Furniture Shop was in 1913 for the Masonic Temple in San Francisco. It consisted of complete interiors for the six lodge rooms and the reception areas, each having its own particular emphasis within the unified style. Done under sub-contract to the architectural firm of Bliss and Faville, the project included large murals, carved and painted architectural embellishments, imposing ceremonial furniture and graceful occasional furniture. In addition, the commission involved specially designed fixtures and the selection of carpets and color schemes. Lucia collaborated with Arthur on many aspects of this decoration. The richly carved and illuminated facing panel to the organ loft in the Blue Lodge meeting room was her own work. Many other interior design projects of this type were executed for private homes, clubs, banks, offices and libraries in the Bay Area.

The second furniture category is the most highly individualistic. These were the truly unique pieces upon which they lavished the magnificent decorations that brought them to the level of masterworks

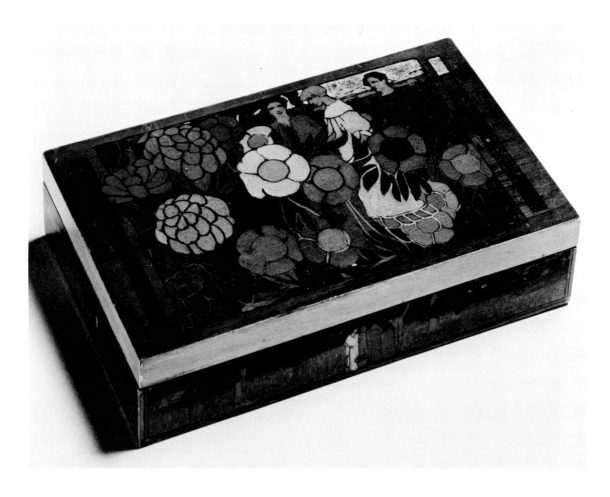

(cat. no. 146)
Lucia K. Mathews
Rectangular Box with Lid

of decorative art. Among the delightfully ornate pieces in the personalized mode were piano cases, cabinets, chests, desks, tables and chairs.

Even within the wide range of styles, each one was only loosely based upon historical models. Architectural features were a dominant characteristic in Arthur's designs for furniture. This obvious reflection of his early training is common to his style

in general. Here again we see a profusion of classical motifs: adaptations of Grecian columns, friezes, pediments, caryatids and other figural elements. As with the paintings, these themes combined with others— from nature in general to California in particular — to express the highly individual style. In those rare instances when Mathews abandoned the classical ideal in his designs, we can see certain Oriental ten-

86

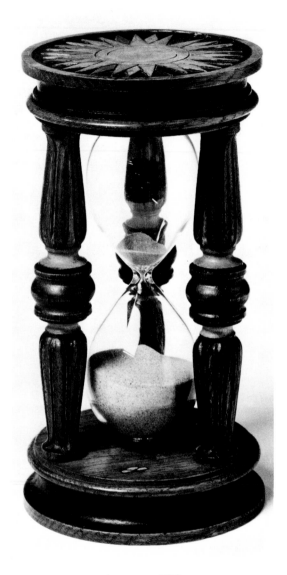

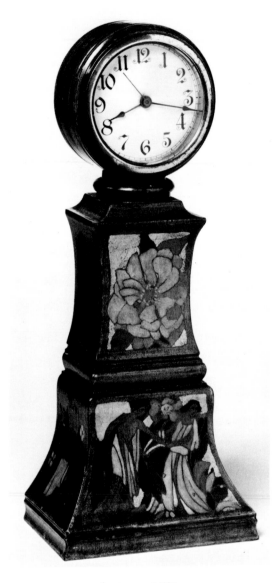

(cat. no. 151)
Arthur F. and Lucia K. Mathews
Hourglass

(cat. no. 150)
Lucia K. Mathews
Clock

dencies. The models of both structural and decorative aspects of Oriental design were easily observed in San Francisco's Chinatown. Moreover, Chinese and Japanese design was a strong influence upon the

functional simplicity so important to Mathews' Arts and Crafts sensibility.

Lucia's emphasis upon the furniture and decorative objects lay in her exquisite use

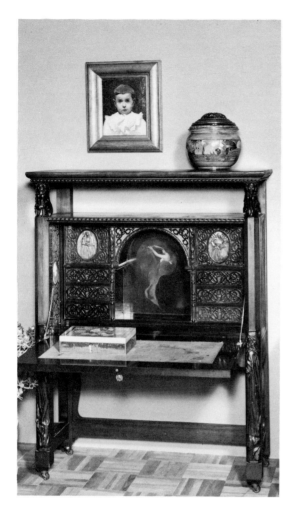

(Cat. nos. 103, 146, 157, 166)
Objects by Furniture Shop,
Arthur F. and Lucia K. Mathews

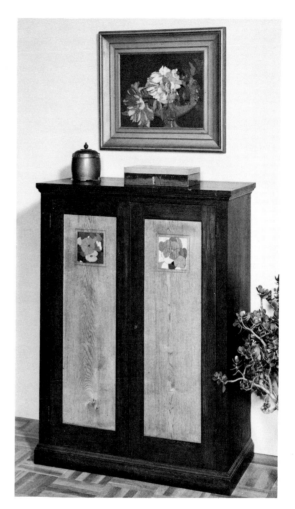

(Cat. nos. 141, 146, 153)
Objects by Furniture Shop
Arthur F. and Lucia K. Mathews

of floral motifs. Much of the surface decoration, both carved and painted, is reminiscent of Oriental prototypes. Among the
many nature motifs in the frame and furniture designs were landscapes, plants,
fruits and flowers common to California:
coastal pine and cypress trees, peaches,
plums, apricots, oranges and grapes, magnolia leaves and flowers, peonies, and a
virtual trademark, the California poppy.

In addition to the floral motifs, some of
the furniture incorporated beautiful oil
paintings and low relief or inlay panels
done in the characteristic figurative style.
Lucia took particular pride in producing
the richly painted and gilded wood accessories that included boxes, candlesticks,
lamps and frames. These belong more in
a category of keepsakes or treasures because they were often created as gifts.

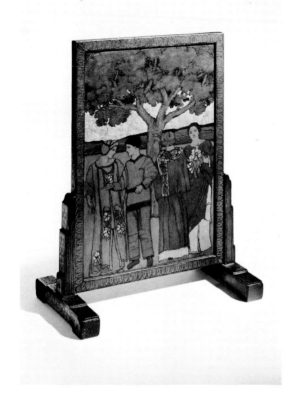

(cat. no. 160)
Lucia K. Mathews
Panel

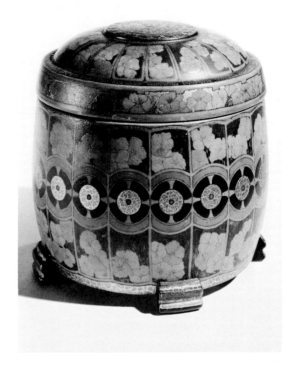

(cat. no. 162)
Lucia K. Mathews
Wooden Jar with Lid

The specially designed picture frames were another important part of Furniture Shop activity. They made what could be called "production" frames from original moldings for rather general application, as well as extremely ornamental or thematic frames created to enhance specific paintings. The latter type constituted frames that were works of art in themselves. It is interesting to note that the Mathewses found it necessary to specially train their woodcarvers to execute the designs in flattened relief; the European trained craftsmen had been accustomed to more fully developed relief forms in their work, and found it difficult to adapt to the Mathews style. Arthur Mathews was very particular about the color of frames intended for his paintings. His rich colors in subdued tones required certain considerations in framing. Mathews' own preference, aside from the individually created frames, was for wide coved moldings finished in a soft textured gray-green color that he found complimentary to the colors of his paintings.

The products of the Furniture Shop were consistently constructed of first-quality

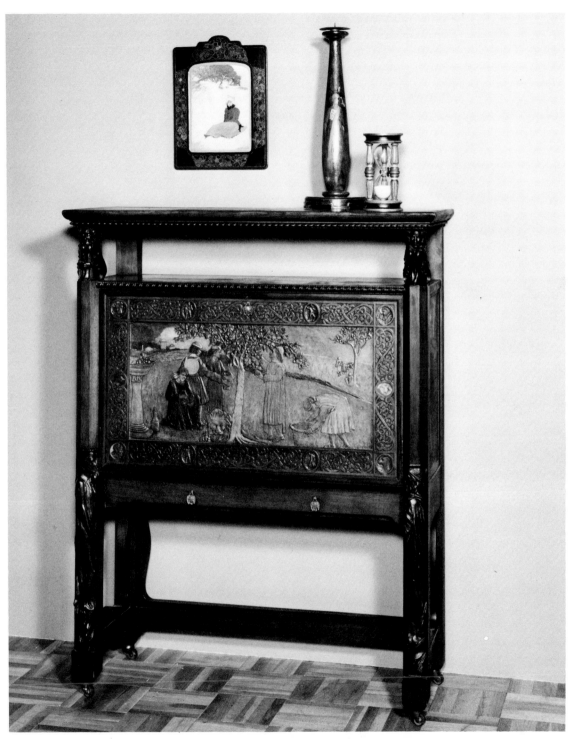

(cat. nos. 113, 147, 151, 166)
Objects by Furniture Shop
Arthur F. and Lucia K. Mathews

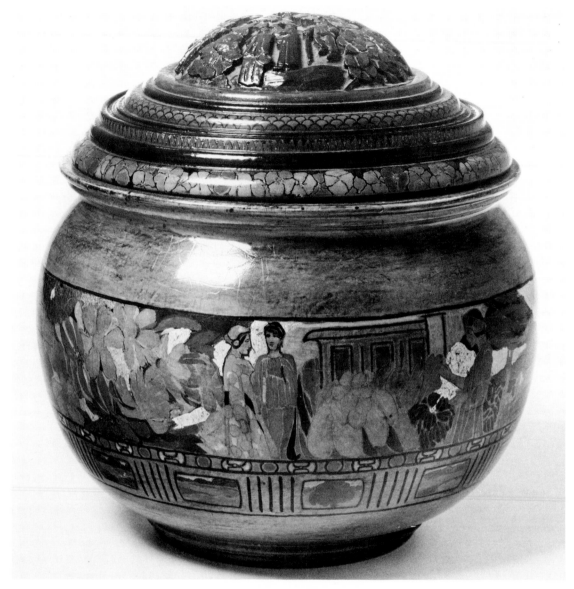

(cat. no. 157)
Arthur F. and Lucia K. Mathews
Wooden Jar with Lid

materials. The wood used included oak, mahogany, beech and pine as well as the more exotic woods selected for inlay work. Emphasis was placed upon functional simplicity. Utilitarian aspects were not sacrificed for decorative effect in spite of certain elaborately decorated surfaces on some pieces. The custom finishes ranged from highly polished dark stains to a blond oak which was used on a very simple "modernistic" style that was some twenty-five years ahead of its popular use in home

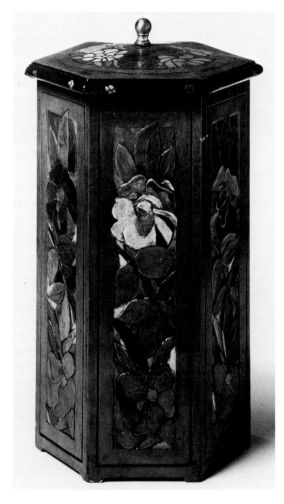

(cat. no. 140)
Lucia K. Mathews
Hexagonal Box with Lid

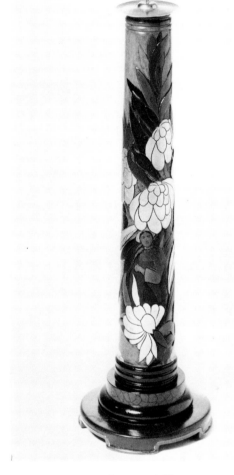

(cat. no. 148)
Arthur F. and Lucia K. Mathews
Cylindrical Candlestick

decoration during the nineteen forties and fifties.

The design and construction was in the highest tradition of handcrafted furniture. Special consideration for function and the honest use of materials were features of Mathews' furniture that owed little else stylistically to the Mission style of Gustav Stickley.

By the time the Furniture Shop closed its doors in 1920, it was said to have netted over a million dollars. Two factors which brought an end to this successful venture were Mathews' advancing age and the U.S. involvement in World War I (1917-1918) when workmen and materials were scarce. During the height of production the furniture and decorations from that shop commanded the admiration of patrons and connoisseurs alike.

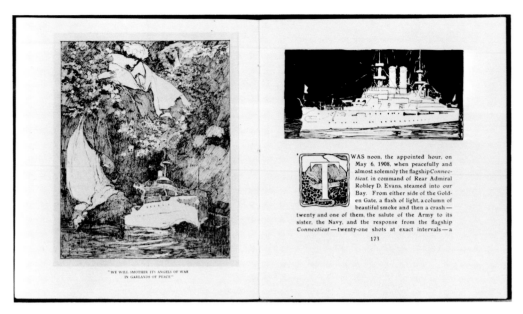

A page from *Philopolis Magazine* May 25, 1908

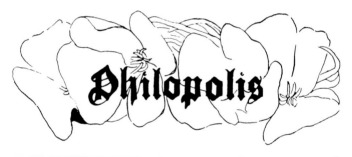

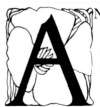ANOTHER aspect of Mathews' activity that received impetus from the 1906 disaster is *Philopolis*. Later that same year, Arthur and Lucia Mathews collaborated with others in the launching of a new monthly magazine devoted to art and city planning, "published for those who care." Its intent was clearly outlined on the first page of the early issues: "It is the purpose of *Philopolis* to consider the ethical and artistic aspects of the rebuilding of San Francisco. We want good art, good architecture, and as a necessity to gain the end, a good civic administration. This is important. As the name implies, *Philopolis* is a friend of the City." Other early associates in this publication were John Zeile, William Sparks and Frederick J. Teggart. At times, during the ten years this little magazine appeared, the list of contributors of signed articles grew to more than twenty. The first few issues were published by the Sequoia Press on Howard Street; then later issues show publication by Philopolis Press at the California Street address of the Furniture Shop. Each copy sold for ten cents and the yearly subscriptions were a dollar.

Arthur Mathews was by far the most prolific contributor, in both writing and illustrations. The many unsigned articles in the magazine bear his writing style. In *Philopolis* he found a voice by which he could influence public opinion in matters of city planning. *Philopolis* reproduced plans and designs that Arthur proposed for various civic improvements, some of which were far reaching. Among his ideas for rebuilding San Francisco were plans to place City Hall on Nob Hill. At other times he envisioned a library and even the Panama-Pacific International Exposition in that prime location. He was both critic and promoter of the plans of others and used his magazine to that effect.

The little magazine was well illustrated and occasionally included photographic reproductions of paintings in color—usually his own. The pages of *Philopolis* were carefully designed and embellished with original decorative initials and floral vignettes by Arthur or Lucia. The general format, typography and layout of *Philopolis* bears a certain resemblance to another little pocket magazine then in national circulation called *The Philistine*. This was Elbert Hubbard's "periodical of protest" that first appeared in 1895. Its basic theme had little involvement in aesthetics but a considerable amount of Hubbard's homely moralizing and wit.

Philopolis continued to publish until its tenth year in 1916. During these years the articles and essays shifted their emphasis from city planning in the rebuilding years, toward more interest in art and politics in that period which preceded the Panama-Pacific International Exposition in 1915.

Concurrently with *Philopolis* magazine, the Philopolis Press was created and operater by Zeile and Mathews from the same location. It published books by various authors of collected essays or poems, as well as some larger works on art or California subjects. Philopolis Press specialized in the production of private limited editions printed from hand-set types on hand-made paper, illustrated with photographs and drawings. Outstanding features of these books were Arthur's and Lucia's elaborate decorative initials and vignettes used in the texts. The added interest of custom bindings, with appropriate original designs stamped in gold, made their books collectors' items.

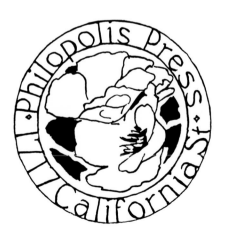

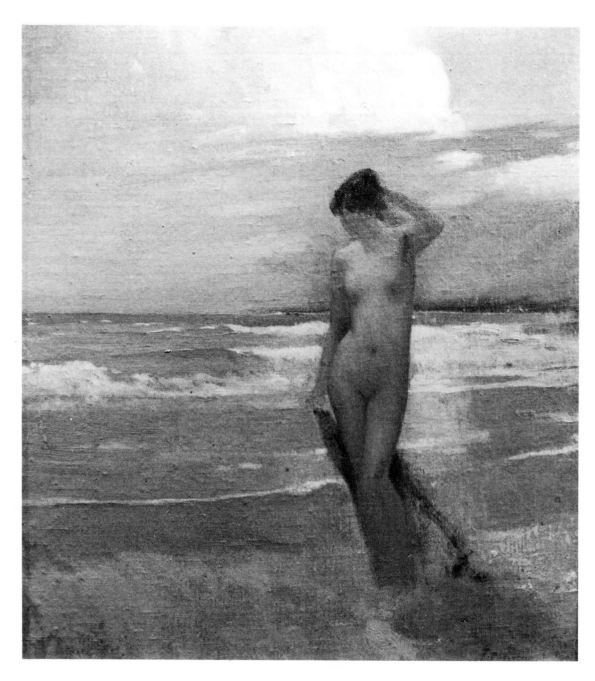

Arthur F. Mathews
Lady on Ocean Beach

Epilogue

ARTHUR AND LUCIA MATHEWS REMEMBERED

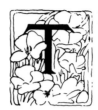

THOSE who personally knew Arthur and Lucia Mathews share fond memories of this remarkable couple. For the rest of us it is through their works that we can begin to realize the unique Mathews vision of art and living. Their long lives were richly rewarding and successful by most standards. They were both respected and influential figures in the community. That they have been relatively unknown outside California is owing to the general unavailability of their works beyond the Bay area. Arthur Mathews was unwilling to leave his home territory in order to extend his sphere of operations. The Mathews popularity was eroded largely by changing artistic taste and passing time.

Arthur Mathews has been characterized as an old time Yankee individualist. His reputation for being mildly contumelious was apparently well earned. A man firmly convinced of his own worth, he held unshakable views on practically any subject. Contemporary accounts from his teaching years suggested that his occasionally brusque manner and caustic remarks were patterned after Whistler.

Lucia Mathews was a quiet modest woman, but was by no means weak in character. She was usually supportive of Arthur's views, although no doubt exerted some influence of her own. Her artistic abilities were what brought her to the attention of Arthur Mathews. Upon his insistence Lucia was placed in the advanced drawing class at the Mark Hopkins Institute over the objections of the other more procedure conscious instructors — she later became his private student. Arthur and Lucia's subsequent marriage was the beginning of a long individual and collaborative artist production. For reasons of their own, they chose not to have children. The many beautiful things they created were the result of disciplined and dignified imaginations that were at once both intellectual and romantic. Arthur Mathews would have doubtless disapproved of the analysis of the California Decorative style that has been attempted here. Like many artists he was reluctant to admit influences and seldom discussed his art in analytical terms. Once during an interview he condemned what he called "the jargon of modern art." In another interview Mathews said his idea of a useless person is the average art critic.

Both Arthur and Lucia possessed prodigious creative energy. They were diligent workers. Even in his later years Arthur worked in his studio every morning for four hours; eight-hour days were common in his youth. He and Lucia maintained separate studios in various locations throughout the years. A housekeeper freed Lucia of many duties at home and allowed her to pursue her own professional interests.

Their visits to Monterey were informal social occasions that provided relaxation and often yielded sketches for paintings and designs.

Friend's memories of the Mathewses included those of Lucia at the wheel of Arthur's Stutz automobile, in which it was said he rode in the back seat but never drove, and recollections of Arthur's life-long smoking habit — he was almost never seen without a roll-your-own cigarette that was his virtual trademark. Lucia's gardening and her prized cactus blossoms, that she captured in watercolor studies, were an important part of her life. Her friendship with John McLaren, the Golden Gate Park landscape architect, resulted in her taking credit for the placement of "Portals of the Past" at his request.

Both Mathews took an interest in several civic and art associations. Arthur was a member of the Bohemian Club and Lucia was active in the Sketch Club. They shared a fondness of music—Lucia played the piano, and she and Arthur regularly attended concerts. Their social circle included many artists and business associates whom they graciously entertained at festive parties at home or in the Furniture Shop studios.

Aside from the frequent trips to Monterey, and two trips to Europe (one for Lucia), they spent most of their productive lives in San Francisco where they made their home in the Fell Street house which had previously belonged to Lucia's family.

Arthur and Lucia Mathews' life's work as artists remains a legacy of beautiful art for which they well deserve to be remembered.

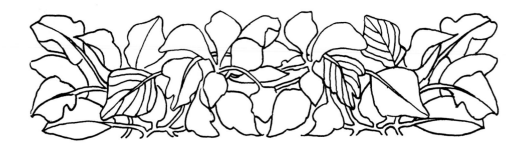

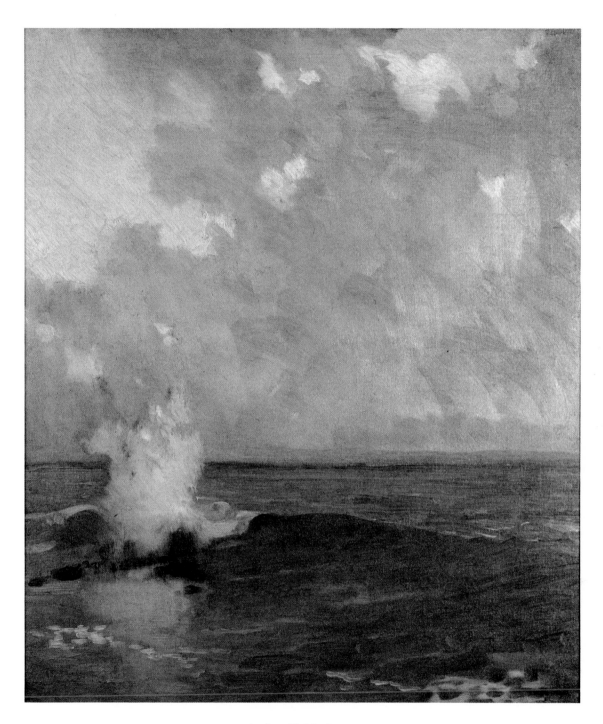

Arthur F. Mathews
Marine

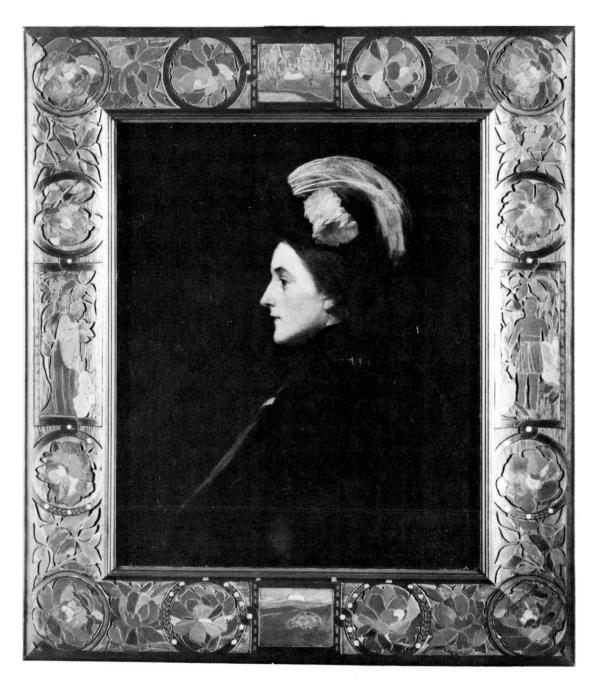

(cat. no. 16)
Arthur F. Mathews
Portrait of Miss Louise Schwamm, 1899

I MATHEWS

Boynton, Ray, "Arthur F. Mathews, Institute Gold Medalist in Painting, 1923," *Journal of the American Institute of Architects*, XI, April 1923, 131-133.

Hailey, Gene, ed., "Arthur Mathews . . . Biography and Works," in *California Art Research Monographs*, VII, (Works Progress Administration, California), San Francisco, 1937, 1-30.

"House Decoration in San Francisco; Arthur F. Mathews," *The Mark Hopkins Institute Review of Art*, I, December 1901, 9-17.

The Oakland Museum: Art Division, Mathews archival material, compiled by the Volunteer Art Research Committee.

Philopolis, I-X, October 1906-September 1916.

M., E. A., "Arthur Mathews, Painter," *Journal of the American Institute of Architects*, VIII, June 1920, 214-216.

Mathews, Arthur F., "In the Fine-Arts Building," *The Californian Illustrated Magazine*, V, March 1894, 409-412.

(Mathews, Arthur F.), "In Deutschland . . . Mathews Gossips of Art; He Speaks of the Result to Art of Students Making a Home Across the Sea," San Francisco *Call*, August 6, 1893, 6.

West, George P., "Secluded S. F. Artist Revealed As State's Leading Mural Painter," San Francisco *Call-Post*, March 28, 1925, second section, 1, 28.

II GENERAL

Art in California, with essays by various contributors, San Francisco, R. L. Bernier, 1916.

California, University of, Davis (Art Department), *Fifteen and Fifty: California Painting at the 1915 Panama-Pacific International Exposition, San Francisco, on its 50th Anniversary*, exhibition catalogue, Davis, California, 1965.

Corn, Wanda M., *The Color of Mood: American Tonalism, 1880-1910*, exhibition catalogue, M. H. De Young Memorial Museum and the California Palace of the Legion of Honor, San Francisco, 1972.

Ferbraché, Lewis, *Theodore Wores — Artist in Search of the Picturesque*, privately printed, Alameda, California, David Printing Co., 1968.

Hall, Kate Montague, "The Mark Hopkins Institute of Art, a Department of the University of California," *Overland Monthly*, XXX, December 1897, 539-548.

Neuhaus, Eugen, *Art of the Exposition*, San Francisco, Paul Elder & Co., 1915.

——————, *History and Ideals of American Art*, Stanford University, California, Stanford University Press, 1931.

——————, *Painters, Pictures and the People*, San Francisco, Philopolis Press, 1918.

Seavey, Kent L., Exhibition Curator, and various contributors, *A Century of California Painting, 1870-1970; an Exhibition Sponsored by Crocker-Citizens National Bank in Commemoration of its One Hundredth Anniversary*, San Francisco, 1970.

MATHEWS

Masterpieces of the California Decorative Style

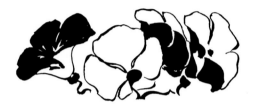

Catalogue

The following listing of works by Arthur and Lucia Mathews was taken from the catalogue of the exhibition organized by The Oakland Museum in 1972. It represents a comprehensive survey of most major paintings, furniture and decorative objects known to exist in both public and private collections at the present time. Additional listings of murals extant by Arthur Mathews and imprints from Philopolis Press are included in this 1980 edition.

Dimensions are given in inches unless otherwise indicated: height precedes width precedes depth.

The listings are grouped by artist under the name at the top of the page. The Furniture Shop group lists the Mathews collaborative works.

Locations of signatures and dates are indicated when appropriate.
Many Mathews works are unsigned and not dated. When dates for works can be ascertained with reasonable accuracy they are indicated by ca. (circa or about), otherwise a date is not indicated.

1. *Landscape — Paris,* 1886, oil on wood panel 10 x 12, signed bottom right.
   Frame: Furniture Shop; foliage design, carved and stained wood 16¾ x 20¾.
   Collection of The Oakland Museum (65.13.19),
   Gift of Concours d'Antiques, Art Guild, The Oakland Museum Association.

2. *Portrait of a Young Gentleman,* 1886, oil on wood panel 9¾ x 7⅝, signed
   top left. *Plate page 54.*
   Frame: Furniture Shop; fruit and foliage design, carved and stained wood
   15 x 13.
   Collection of The Oakland Museum (66.196.5),
   Gift of Concours d'Antiques, Art Guild, The Oakland Museum Association.

3. *Imogen and Arviragus,* 1887, oil on canvas 34½ x 46½, signed bottom right.
   Plate page 55.
   Frame: Furniture Shop; painted wood 37¼ x 52.
   Collection of The Oakland Museum (65.13.1),
   Gift of Concours d'Antiques, Art Guild, The Oakland Museum Association.

4. *Reclining Woman in Red Dress Reading,* ca. 1887, oil on wood panel
   8⅜ x 10⅜, signed bottom right.
   Frame: Furniture Shop; fruit and foliage design, carved and stained wood
   13¼ x 15¼.
   Collection of The Oakland Museum (65.13.21),
   Gift of Concours d'Antiques, Art Guild, The Oakland Museum Association.

5. *Paris Studio Interior,* ca. 1887, oil on canvasboard 20 x 24, signed bottom
   left. *Plate page 68.*
   Frame: Furniture Shop; floral design with male and female figures, carved
   wood 35 x 39½.
   Collection of The Oakland Museum (65.13.17),
   Gift of Concours d'Antiques, Art Guild, The Oakland Museum Association.

6. *Woman Bathing,* oil on wood panel 10 x 8, signed to right.
   Frame: Furniture Shop; fruit and foliage design, carved and stained wood
   15¼ x 13¼.
   Collection of The Oakland Museum (65.13.22),
   Gift of Concours d'Antiques, Art Guild, The Oakland Museum Association.

7. *The Lilies of Midas,* 1888, oil on canvas 28¼ x 39¼, signed bottom left.
   Plate page 18.
   Extended loan to The Oakland Museum (EL60.20.105),
   Courtesy of the M. H. de Young Memorial Museum,
   Gift of Mrs. Henrietta Zeile.

8. *Eve,* oil on canvas mounted on wood panel 50½ x 38, no signature. *Plate page 42.*
   Frame: Furniture Shop; allegorical figures, floral and fruit designs, land-
     scapes with figures by Lucia, carved and painted wood 66 x 53½.
   Collection of The Oakland Museum (66.196.9),
   Gift of Concours d'Antiques, Art Guild, The Oakland Museum Association.

9. *The Butterfly,* oil on canvas 26 x 88½, signed bottom right. *Plate page 60.*
   Frame: Furniture Shop; painted wood 36 x 32.
   Collection of The Oakland Museum (65.13.6),
   Gift of Concours d'Antiques, Art Guild, The Oakland Museum Association.

10. *The Web* (The Three Fates), oil on canvas 26½ x 23¼, signed bottom
    right. *Plate page 57.*
    Frame: Furniture Shop; corner floral designs, carved and painted wood
      37½ x 34½, poppy hallmark.
    Collection of The Oakland Museum (66.196.1),
    Gift of Concours d'Antiques, Art Guild, The Oakland Museum Association.

11. *Two Figures,* oil on canvas 26 x 22½, signed bottom left. *Plate page 72.*
    Frame: Furniture Shop: floral design, carved and painted wood 34 x 30.
    Collection of The Oakland Museum (65.13.7),
    Gift of Concours d'Antiques, Art Guild, The Oakland Museum Association.

12. *Portrait of Pauline Marie Mathews,* oil on canvas 45½ x 30½, signed
    bottom right.
    Lent by Mr. and Mrs. Edwin Oetinger, Chico, California.

13. *Portrait of Woman in Park* (study for "Picnic at El Campo"), 1893, oil
    on wood panel 18 x 12⅝, signed bottom right.
    Collection of The Oakland Museum (65.13.20),
    Gift of Concours d'Antiques, Art Guild, The Oakland Museum Association.

14. *Discovery of the Bay of San Francisco by Portola,* 1896, oil on canvas
    70¼ x 58½, signed bottom left. *Plate page 21.*
    Frame: Furniture Shop; fruit and leaf design with panels of figures in
      landscape, fluted and floral borders; painted, gold-leafed and carved
      wood 85 x 73.
    John H. Garzoli Fine Arts, San Francisco.

15. *Portrait of John Zeile,* oil on canvas 33 x 28, signed bottom right.
    Frame: Furniture Shop; fluting and foliage design, carved and painted
      wood 39 x 33¾.
    Extended loan to The Oakland Museum (EL60.20.80),
    Courtesy of the M. H. de Young Memorial Museum,
    Gift of Mrs. Henrietta Zeile.

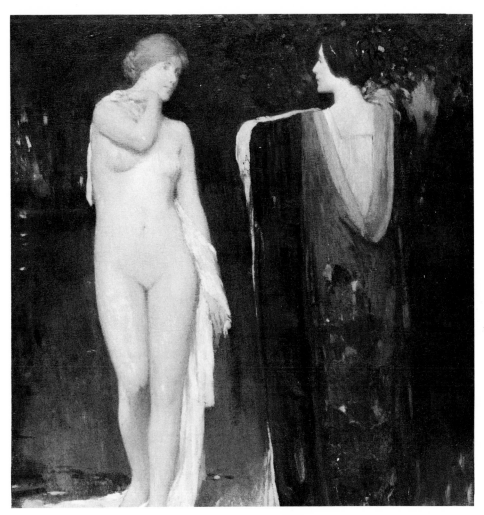

(cat. no. 21)
Arthur F. Mathews
Art and Nature

16. *Portrait of Miss Louise Schwamm,* 1899, oil on canvas 28 x 23½, signed bottom right. *Plate page 98.*
Frame: Furniture Shop; floral medallions, rectangles with landscapes and figures, carved and painted wood 39½ x 35.
Collection of The Oakland Museum (66.196.10),
Gift of Concours d'Antiques, Art Guild, The Oakland Museum Association.

17. *Portrait of Lucia Mathews,* ca. 1899, oil on canvas 14 x 12, no signature. *Plate page 81.*
Frame: Furniture Shop; painted wood 25½ x 23½.
Collection of The Oakland Museum (66.196.14),
Gift of Concours d'Antiques, Art Guild, The Oakland Museum Association.

18. *Portrait of Lucia Mathews,* ca. 1899, oil on canvas 14 x 12, no signature.
    Collection of The Oakland Museum (66.196.25),
    Gift of Concours d'Antiques, Art Guild, The Oakland Museum Association.

19. *Portrait of Lucia Mathews in Pink Robe,* ca. 1899, oil on wood panel
    17¼ x 14, no signature.
    Lent by Mrs. Margaret R. Kleinhans, San Francisco.

20. *The Swan,* oil on canvas 26 x 23, signed bottom left. *Plate page 60.*
    Frame: Furniture Shop; floral design, carved and painted wood 38½ x 35½,
        poppy hallmark.
    Collection of The Oakland Museum (65.13.14),
    Gift of Concours d'Antiques, Art Guild, The Oakland Museum Association.

21. *Art and Nature,* oil on canvas, 30 x 26, no signature. *Plate page 103.*
    Frame: Furniture Shop; fish scale motif, painted wood 33¼ x 29⅛.
    Collection of The Oakland Museum (66.196.16),
    Gift of Concours d'Antiques, Art Guild, The Oakland Museum Association.

22. *Mandarin Robe,* oil on canvas 26 x 23, no signature. *Plate page 71.*
    Frame: Furniture Shop; painted wood 33 x 29¾.
    Collection of The Oakland Museum (66.196.3),
    Gift of Concours d'Antiques, Art Guild, The Oakland Museum Association.

23. *The Wave,* oil on canvas 25½ x 22½, signed bottom left. *Plate page 70.*
    Collection of The Oakland Museum (66.196.8),
    Gift of Concours d'Antiques, Art Guild, The Oakland Museum Association.

24. *Cypress Grove,* 1903, oil on canvas 48 x 52, signed bottom right.
    Frame: Furniture Shop; dragon and floral design, carved and painted wood
        64 x 68. *Plate page 105.*
    Collection of The Oakland Museum (66.196.7),
    Gift of Concours d'Antiques, Art Guild, The Oakland Museum Association.

25. *Monterey Cypress,* ca. 1904, oil on canvas 26 x 30, signed bottom right.
    Plate page 9.
    Lent by The Metropolitan Museum of Art,
    Gift of Mrs. John Zeile, 1909.

26. *The Grape,* oil on canvas 26 x 24⅛, signed bottom right. *Plate page 69.*
    Frame: Furniture Shop; poppy and medallion design, carved and painted
        wood 40½ x 37.
    Extended loan to The Oakland Museum (EL60.20.8),
    Courtesy of the M. H. de Young Memorial Museum,
    Gift of Mrs. Henrietta Zeile.

27. *California,* 1905, oil on canvas 26 x 23½, no signature. *Plate page 11.*
    Frame: Furniture Shop; classical motifs with floral designs, carved and
        painted wood 47½ x 38.
    Collection of The Oakland Museum (66.196.4),
    Gift of Concours d'Antiques, Art Guild, The Oakland Museum Association.

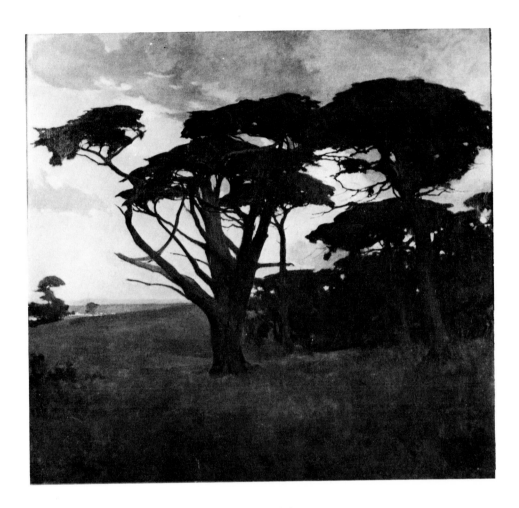

(cat. no. 24)
Arthur F. Mathews
Cypress Grove, 1903

28. *Monterey Beach,* oil on canvas 26½ x 37⅛, signed bottom right. *Plate page 64*.
Frame: Furniture Shop; painted wood 38½ x 39¼.
Collection of The Oakland Museum (66.196.26),
Gift of Concours d'Antiques, Art Guild, The Oakland Museum Association.

29. *Monterey Landscape,* oil on wood panel 22 x 25, no signature.
Frame: Furniture Shop; painted wood 28½ x 31½.
Collection of The Oakland Museum (65.13.3),
Gift of Concours d'Antiques, Art Guild, The Oakland Museum Association.

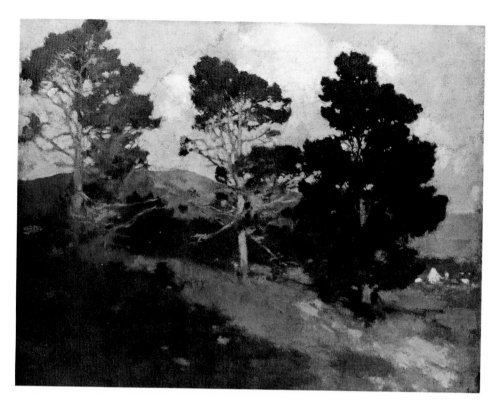

(cat. no. 48)
Arthur F. Mathews
Monterey Pines

30. *Three Women at the Beach,* oil on wood panel 18½ x 12, signed bottom right. *Plate page 26.*
Frame: Furniture Shop; carved and stained wood 26¾ x 12.
Lent by the California Palace of the Legion of Honor,
Gift from the collection of May and Paul Sinsheimer.

31. *Masque of Pandora,* 1914-1915, oil on canvas 52 x 48, signed bottom left. *Plate page 35.*
Frame: Furniture Shop; Egyptian motifs, carved and painted wood 67 x 63.
Collection of The Oakland Museum (66.196.11),
Gift of Concours d'Antiques, Art Guild, The Oakland Museum Association.

32. *Sacred and Profane Love,* 1915, oil on canvas 38½ x 50¾, signed bottom right. *Plate page 38.*
Frame: Furniture Shop; classical motifs with poppy and floral designs, carved and painted wood 54½ x 67¾.
Collection of The Oakland Museum (66.196.19),
Gift of Concours d'Antiques, Art Guild, The Oakland Museum Association.

33. *View From Skyline Boulevard, San Francisco,* 1915, oil on canvas 30 x 40,
signed bottom left. *Plate page 59.*
Collection of The Oakland Museum (72.8.2),
Gift of Concours d'Antiques, Art Guild, The Oakland Museum Association.

34. *A Masque,* oil on canvas mounted on wood panel 39¾ x 29, no signature.
Plate page 26.
Frame: Furniture Shop; painted wood 43½ x 33¾.
Collection of The Oakland Museum (65.13.2),
Gift of Concours d'Antiques, Art Guild, The Oakland Museum Association.

35. *I Piped But Ye Would Not Dance,* oil on canvas 50½ x 38¾, no signature.
Plate page 36.
Frame: Furniture Shop; classical motifs with border of draped figures,
carved and painted wood 66¼ x 53½.
Collection of the Hirshhorn Museum and Sculpture Garden.

36. *Water Queen,* oil on canvas 30 x 26, no signature. *Plate page 10.*
Collection of The Oakland Museum (65.13.15),
Gift of Concours d'Antiques, Art Guild, The Oakland Museum Association.

37. *Dancing Girls,* oil on canvas 38 x 50, no signature. *Plate page 73.*
Collection of The Oakland Museum (66.196.12),
Gift of Concours d'Antiques, Art Guild, The Oakland Museum Association.

38. *Youth,* ca. 1917, oil on canvas 38 x 50, signed bottom left. *Cover Plate.*
Frame: Furniture Shop; classical and animal motifs with poppy and floral
designs, carved and painted wood 59½ x 67¾.
Collection of The Oakland Museum (66.196.24),
Gift of Concours d'Antiques, Art Guild, The Oakland Museum Association.

39. *Dancing Figures,* 1917, oil on canvas, 34 x 52¾, signed bottom right.
John H. Garzoli Fine Arts, San Francisco.   *Plate page 63.*

40. *Dancing Girls,* oil on canvas 29½ x 39½, no signature. *Plate page 40.*
Collection of The Oakland Museum (66.196.22),
Gift of Concours d'Antiques, Art Guild, The Oakland Museum Association.

41. *The Dancers,* oil on wood panel 19 x 22¼, signed bottom right. *Plate
page 44.*
Lent by the Monterey Peninsula Museum of Art,
Collection of the City of Monterey.

42. *Dancing Girls on Carmel Beach,* oil on canvas 26¼ x 22¼, signed bottom
left. *Plate page 49.*
Frame: Furniture Shop; floral designs, carved and painted wood 36¾ x 33.
Lent by Mr. and Mrs. Anthony R. White, Hillsborough.

43. *David and Bathsheba,* oil on canvas 34 x 38, no signature.
Lent by Mr. Edgar M. Sliney, San Rafael.

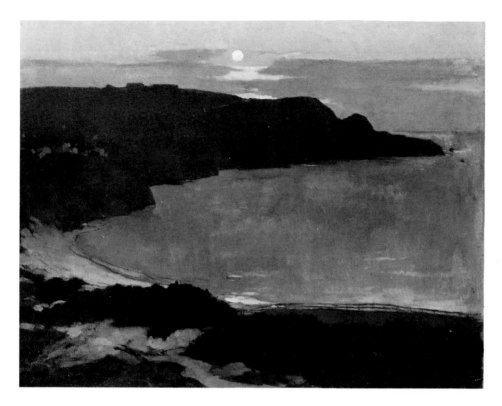

(cat. no. 52)
Arthur F. Mathews
Land's End

44. *Satyr and Nymph,* oil on canvas 30 x 26, no signature. *Plate page 43.*
    Frame: Furniture Shop; cypress tree motif, painted wood 43½ x 39½, no
    signature.
    Lent by Mr. Edgar M. Sliney, San Rafael.

45. *The Berkeley Hills,* 1925, oil on canvas 52 x 48½, signed bottom right.
    Lent by Mr. and Mrs. Czar Smith Winters, San Rafael.

46. *Ladies on the Grass,* oil on canvas 48 x 52, no signature. *Plate page 47.*
    Lent by Mr. and Mrs. Robert Crutchfield, San Francisco.

47. *Ladies Dancing on the Lawn,* oil on canvas 51½ x 47½, no signature.
    Lent by Mrs. Anthony R. White, Hillsborough.

48. *Monterey Pines,* oil on canvas 23 x 26, no signature. *Plate page 106.*
    Collection of The Oakland Museum (66.196.18),
    Gift of Concours d'Antiques, Art Guild, The Oakland Museum Association.

49. *Carmel Valley,* oil on canvas 22 x 26, no signature.
    Collection of The Oakland Museum (65.113.13),
    Gift of Concours d'Antiques, Art Guild, The Oakland Museum Association.

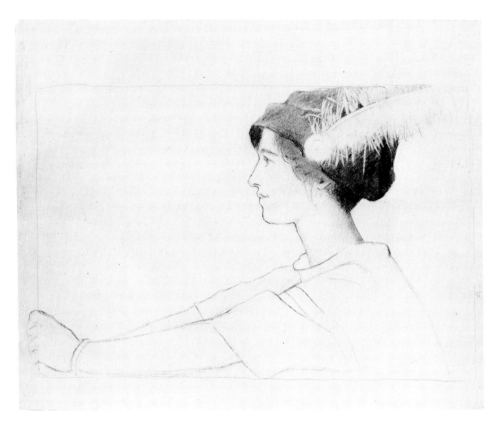

(cat. no. 112)
Lucia K. Mathews
Girl with Feathered Cap

50. *Monterey Oaks,* oil on canvas 23 x 26, no signature.
 Frame: Furniture Shop; double human profiles in four corners, carved
  and painted wood 34¼ x 38.
 Collection of The Oakland Museum (66.196.17),
 Gift of Concours d'Antiques, Art Guild, The Oakland Museum Association.

51. *Landscape — San Francisco,* oil on canvas 26 x 30, no signature. *Plate
 page 37.*
 Frame: Furniture Shop; cypress tree motif, painted wood 39¾ x 43½.
 Collection of the Oakland Museum (65.13.9),
 Gift of Concours d'Antiques, Art Guild, The Oakland Museum Association.

52. *Land's End,* oil on canvas 26½ x 30, no signature. *Plate page 108.*
 Lent by Mr. Edgar M. Sliney, San Rafael.

53. *Summer Day,* 1930, oil on wood panel 14 x 12½, signed bottom right.
 Collection of The Oakland Museum (65.13.18),
 Gift of Concours d'Antiques, Art Guild, The Oakland Museum Association.

54. *Monterey Cypress,* 1930, oil on canvas 25½ x 29½, signed bottom right. Frame: Furniture Shop; cypress tree motif, painted wood 39¾ x 43½. Collection of The Oakland Museum (66.196.2),   *Plate page 65.* Gift of Concours d'Antiques, Art Guild, The Oakland Museum Association.

55. *Monterey Cypress,* 1930, oil on canvas 38 x 34, signed bottom right. Frame: Furniture Shop; cypress tree motif, painted wood 48 x 44. Collection of The Oakland Museum (66.196.21), Gift of Concours d'Antiques, Art Guild, The Oakland Museum Association.

56. *Monterey Cypress,* 1933, oil on canvas 38¼ x 34¼, signed bottom right. Frame: Furniture Shop; fish scale motif, painted wood 48 x 44. Collection of The Oakland Museum (66.196.15),   *Plate page 41.* Gift of Concours d'Antiques, Art Guild, The Oakland Museum Association.

57. *View of the Knights Templar Parade in San Francisco, August 20th, 1883. Souvenir of 22nd Triennial Conclave, K.T.,* 1883, lithograph on paper 15½ x 23¼ (Imp.), printed by Britton & Rey, Lithographers, San Francisco, signed bottom right. *Plate page 17.* Lent by the California Historical Society, San Francisco, Gift of Mr. Albert Bender.

58. *San Francisco Souvenir — Front page to the Knight Templar's Grand Entree March by Henry Marsh,* 1883, lithograph on paper 13¼ x 9¾ (Imp.), printed by Britton & Rey, Lithographers, San Francisco, signed bottom left. Collection of The Oakland Museum (72.10c), Gift of Anonymous Donor.

59. *Street Urchin,* 1891, pastel on paper 25 x 19, signed bottom right. Lent by Mr. Edgar M. Sliney, San Rafael.

60. *Landscape — Oak Trees and Hills,* pastel on paper 9½ x 11½, signed bottom right. Lent by Mr. and Mrs. Edwin Oetinger, Chico.

61. *Landscape,* pastel on paper 10 x 13, no signature. Collection of The Oakland Museum (65.13.97), Gift of Concours d'Antiques, Art Guild, The Oakland Museum Association.

62. *Seascape,* pastel on paper 10 x 12¾, no signature. Collection of The Oakland Museum (65.13.77), Gift of Concours d'Antiques, Art Guild, The Oakland Museum Association.

63. *Landscape with Two Oaks,* pastel on paper 10 x 12¾, no signature. Collection of The Oakland Museum (65.13.72), Gift of Concours d'Antiques, Art Guild, The Oakland Museum Association.

64. *Landscape with Oaks and Eucalyptus,* pastel on paper 10 x 12¾, no signature. Collection of The Oakland Museum (65.13.66), Gift of Concours d'Antiques, Art Guild, The Oakland Museum Association.

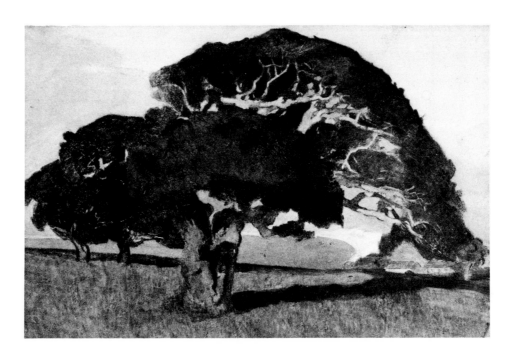

(cat. no. 115)
Lucia K. Mathews
Monterey Oak

65. *Sketch for "The Arts,"* gouache on paper 26½ x 16¼ (sight), no signature.
Lent by Mr. and Mrs. Anthony R. White, Hillsborough.

66. *As a Youth,* 1907, gouache, pencil, ink on paper 19¼ x 15¾, signed bottom left.
Collection of The Oakland Museum (62.89.8),
Gift of Mr. L. E. Ferbraché.

67. *Harbor Scene,* watercolor on paper 13¼ x 21¾ (lunette) (sight), signed bottom right.
Lent by Mr. Thomas A. McGlynn, Jr., San Francisco.

68. *Invitation for Mardi Gras Bal Masque, Mark Hopkins Institute of Art,* 1905, ink on paperboard 7⅛ x 5, signed bottom right. *Plate page 22.*
Collection of The Oakland Museum (65.13.375),
Gift of Concours d'Antiques, Art Guild, The Oakland Museum Association.

69. *Girl with Peacock,* 1906, pencil and watercolor on paper 30 x 22, signed bottom left.
Lent by the Santa Barbara Museum of Art,
Gift of Mr. Harold Wagner.

70. *Two Youths,* pencil on paper 32 x 23¾, no signature.
Lent by the Santa Barbara Museum of Art,
Gift of Mr. Harold Wagner.

71. *1717 California Street* (illustration for *Philopolis*), ink on paperboard 5¾ x 7½, no signature. *Plate page 25.*
Collection of The Oakland Museum (65.13.222),
Gift of Concours d'Antiques, Art Guild, The Oakland Museum Association.

72. *Dante and Beatrice,* ca. 1910, (illustration for *Philopolis*), gouache on paper 17 x 15 (sight), signed bottom right.
Lent by Dr. and Mrs. Bruce Friedman, Piedmont.

73. *Dancing Figures,* 1910, gouache on paper 36¾ x 53¾, signed bottom right. *Plate page 120.*
Lent by Dr. and Mrs. Jacob Foster, Salinas.

74. *The City,* 1913, (sketch for mural in the rotunda of California State Capitol, Sacramento), pencil and watercolor on paper 30 x 22, no signature. *Plate page 52.*
Lent by the Santa Barbara Museum of Art,
Gift of Mr. Harold Wagner.

75. *Contemplation,* 1913, (sketch for mural in the rotunda of California State Capitol, Sacramento), pencil and watercolor on paper 30 x 22, no signature.
Lent by the Santa Barbara Museum of Art,
Gift of Mr. Harold Wagner.

76. *The Pioneers,* 1913, (sketch for mural in the rotunda of California State Capitol, Sacramento), pencil and watercolor on paper 30 x 22, no signature.
Lent by the Santa Barbara Museum of Art,
Gift of Mr. Harold Wagner.

77. *Modern City,* 1913, (sketch for mural in the rotunda of California State Capitol, Sacramento), pencil and watercolor on paper 30 x 22, no signature. *Plate page 52.*
Lent by the Santa Barbara Museum of Art,
Gift of Mr. Harold Wagner.

78. *Mission Era,* 1913, (sketch for mural in the rotunda of California State Capitol, Sacramento), pencil and watercolor on paper 30 x 22, no signature.
Lent by the Santa Barbara Museum of Art,
Gift of Mr. Harold Wagner.

79. *Discovery of San Francisco Bay,* 1913, (sketch for mural in the rotunda of California State Capitol, Sacramento), pencil and watercolor on paper 30 x 22, no signature.
Lent by the Santa Barbara Museum of Art,
Gift of Mr. Harold Wagner.

80. *Adventure,* 1913, (sketch for mural in the rotunda of California State Capitol, Sacramento), pencil and watercolor on paper 30 x 22, no signature.
Lent by the Santa Barbara Museum of Art,
Gift of Mr. Harold Wagner.

81. *The Arts of Peace,* 1896, mural (frieze designed for the Horace L. Hill residence, San Francisco), oil on canvas 3' x 108', signed bottom edge.
Collection of The Oakland Museum (70.43a-d),
Gift of John and Ann Ryan.

82. *Nature,* 1904, (for the Oakland Free Library, Charles Greene Branch), oil on canvas 9'9" x 7'9".
Collection of The Oakland Museum,
Lent by the Oakland Public Library.

83. *The Arts,* 1904, (for the Oakland Free Library, Charles Greene Branch), oil on canvas 9'9" x 7'9". *Plate page 6.*
Collection of The Oakland Museum,
Lent by the Oakland Public Library.

84. *Resignation,* 1907, (for the Oakland Free Library, Charles Greene Branch), oil on canvas 9'9" x 7'9". *Plate page 51.*
Collection of The Oakland Museum,
Lent by the Oakland Public Library.

85. *Conquest,* 1907, (for the Oakland Free Library, Charles Greene Branch), oil on canvas 9'9" x 7'9". *Plate page 51.*
Collection of The Oakland Museum,
Lent by the Oakland Public Library

The Soil, 1908, (for the Oakland Free Library, Charles Greene Branch), oil on canvas 8' x 6'.
Collection of the Oakland Public Library.

The Grain, 1908, (for the Oakland Free Library, Charles Green Branch), oil on canvas 8' x 6'.
Collection of the Oakland Public Library.

Health and the Arts (3 panels, *The Medicine Man, Olympus, The Evil Eye*), 1912, (for the Lane Hospital Medical Library) oil on 3 canvases.
Collection of the Pacific Medical Center, Health Sciences Library, San Francisco.

The History of California, 1914, (twelve panels for the rotunda of the California State Capitol, Sacramento), *The Festival, Contemplation, The Temple, The White Wings, The Franciscan, The Discovery of San Francisco Bay, Mexican Period, Spanish Mission Period, The American Occupation of Monterey, The Discovery of Gold, Westward Ho, Modern City,* oil on 12 canvases.
Collection of the State of California.

86. *Untitled* (intended placement unknown), oil on canvas 49" x 80". *Plate page 53.*
Collection of The Oakland Museum,
Gift of Concours d'Antiques, Art Guild, The Oakland Museum Association.

Untitled, 1917, vestibule of the Mechanics' Institute Library, San Francisco, oil on canvas.

87. *Untitled,* 1921, 2 murals for the "catacombs" of Cypress Lawn Cemetery, Colma, California; 2 panels, oil on canvas.

Untitled, 1922, 2 murals for the Curran Theatre, San Francisco; 2 panels, oil on canvas.

88. *The Commonwealth,* 1924, mural sketch (designed for the California Supreme Court, San Francisco), oil on canvas 2' 8¾" x 6' 10", no signature.
Lent by the Santa Barbara Museum of Art,
Gift of Mr. Harold Wagner.

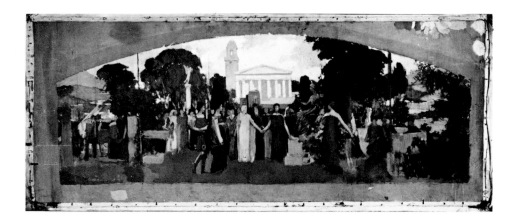

(cat. no. 88)
Arthur F. Mathews
Oil Sketch for Mural

89. *Franc Pierce Hammon Memorial Window*, 1925, (designed for the Women's City Club, San Francisco), leaded stained glass 12′ x 11′, no signature. *Plate page 30.*
Collection of The Oakland Museum,
Gift of Mr. and Mrs. James R. Moore and Family.

90. Photograph of murals in the California State Capitol rotunda (*The City*), black and white photograph by Francis Bruguiere, no signature.
Collection of The Oakland Museum (65.13.286),
Gift of Concours d'Antiques, Art Guild, The Oakland Museum Association.

91. Photograph of murals in the California State Capitol rotunda (*Adventure*), black and white photograph by Francis Bruguiere, no signature.
Collection of The Oakland Museum (65.13.307),
Gift of Concours d'Antiques, Art Guild, The Oakland Museum Association.

92. Photograph of murals in the California State Capitol rotunda (*The American*), black and white photograph by Francis Bruguiere, no signature.
Collection of The Oakland Museum (65.13.308),
Gift of Concours d'Antiques, Art Guild, The Oakland Museum Association.

93. Photograph of murals in the California State Capitol rotunda (*The Missionary*), black and white photograph by Francis Bruguiere, no signature.
Collection of The Oakland Museum (65.13.309),
Gift of Concours d'Antiques, Art Guild, The Oakland Museum Association.

94. *River Seine, Paris,* 1899, oil on paperboard 4 x 6, no signature.
Collection of the Oakland Museum (64.59.23),
Gift of Mr. Harold Wagner.

95. *Park Scene, Paris,* 1899, oil on wood panel 4 x 6, no signature.
Collection of The Oakland Museum (64.59.24),
Gift of Mr. Harold Wagner.

96. *Seated Figures in a Park, Paris,* 1899, oil on paperboard 5¾ x 3⅞, no signature.
Collection of The Oakland Museum (64.59.18),
Gift of Mr. Harold Wagner.

97. *Figures on a Park Bench, Paris,* 1899, oil on paperboard 5¾ x 3⅞, signed bottom left.
Collection of The Oakland Museum (64.59.16),
Gift of Mr. Harold Wagner.

98. *Woman in Hospital, Paris,* 1899, oil on paperboard 5⅞ x 3¼, no signature.
Collection of The Oakland Museum (64.59.13),
Gift of Mr. Harold Wagner.

99. *Beach Scene, France,* 1899, oil on paperboard 3⅞ x 5¾, signed bottom left.
Collection of The Oakland Museum (64.59.21),
Gift of Mr. Harold Wagner.

100. *Sand Dunes and Beach Umbrellas,* 1899, oil on wood panel 10¼ x 8⅝, no signature.
Collection of The Oakland Museum (64.59.99),
Gift of Mr. Harold Wagner.

101. *Self Portrait,* ca. 1899, oil on wood panel 10 x 10⅝, no signature. *Plate page 23.*
Collection of The Oakland Museum (64.59.100),
Gift of Mr. Harold Wagner.

102. *Red and White,* oil on canvas 26 x 19, no signature. *Plate page 49.*
Collection of The Oakland Museum (64.59.141),
Gift of Mr. Harold Wagner.

103. *Portrait of a Young Boy,* oil on wood panel 12 x 9½, signed bottom right. *Plate page 87.*
Frame: Furniture Shop; painted wood 19½ x 17¼,
Collection of The Oakland Museum (64.59.138),
Gift of Mr. Harold Wagner.

104. *Child In White,* oil on canvas 30 x 19, signed bottom right. *Plate page 80.*
Lent by Mills College Art Gallery,
Gift of Mr. Albert M. Bender.

105. *Portrait of a Young Girl in White,* oil on wood panel 10¼ x 8⅝, signed bottom right.
Frame: Furniture Shop; peony design, carved and painted wood 22 x 20¼.
Collection of The Oakland Museum (64.59.135),
Gift of Mr. Harold Wagner.

106. *View Across Hillside*, oil on wood panel 10¼ x 8½, no signature.
Collection of The Oakland Museum (64.59.97),
Gift of Mr. Harold Wagner.

107. *Beach, California*, oil on wood panel 5⅞ x 3⅞, no signature.
Collection of The Oakland Museum (64.59.35),
Gift of Mr. Harold Wagner.

108. *Sand Dunes, California*, oil on wood panel 3⅞ x 5⅞, no signature.
Collection of The Oakland Museum (64.59.33),
Gift of Mr. Harold Wagner.

109. *Scene, Panama-Pacific International Exposition, San Francisco*, 1915, oil on paperboard 5¾ x 3¾, signed bottom left.
Collection of The Oakland Museum (64.59.31),
Gift of Mr. Harold Wagner.

110. *Scene, Panama-Pacific International Exposition, San Francisco*, 1915, oil on wood panel 3⅞ x 5⅞, no signature.
Collection of The Oakland Museum (64.59.4),
Gift of Mr. Harold Wagner.

111. *Scene, Panama-Pacific International Exposition, San Francisco*, 1915, oil on wood panel 5⅞ x 3⅞, no signature.
Collection of The Oakland Museum (64.59.2),
Gift of Mr. Harold Wagner.

112. *Girl with Feathered Cap*, charcoal and pastel on paper 19 x 24½, no signature. *Plate page 109.*
Collection of The Oakland Museum (65.13.195),
Gift of Concours d'Antiques, Art Guild, The Oakland Museum Association.

113. *Seated Girl on Sand Dunes*, 1897, pastel on sandpaper 11¼ x 11½, signed bottom left. *Plate page 78.*
Frame: Furniture Shop; floral design on painted wood 17¾ x 13⅝.
Collection of The Oakland Museum (64.59.103),
Gift of Mr. Harold Wagner.

114. *Woman Sketching*, pastel on paper 13½ x 9½, no signature.
Frame: Furniture Shop; floral design, painted and stained wood 18 x 13½.
Collection of The Oakland Museum (65.13.248),
Gift of Concours d'Antiques, Art Guild, The Oakland Museum Association.

115. *Monterey Oak*, watercolor on paper mounted on canvas 19 x 26, signed bottom right. *Plate page 111.*
Frame: Furniture Shop; carved wood 30¼ x 37½.
Collection of The Oakland Museum (64.59.136),
Gift of Mr. Harold Wagner.

116. *Apricots #1*, 1908, pastel on buff paper 13¼ x 11 (sight), signed bottom right.
Frame: Furniture Shop; fruit and foliage design, carved and stained wood 20½ x 16½.
Collection of The Oakland Museum (64.59.58),
Gift of Mr. Harold Wagner.

117. *Apricots #2*, 1908, watercolor on paper 14 x 11 (sight), dated bottom right.
Collection of The Oakland Museum (64.59.62),
Gift of Mr. Harold Wagner.

118. *Apricots #3*, 1908, pastel on paper 21 x 14, no signature. *Plate page 80.*
Collection of The Oakland Museum (64.59.139),
Gift of Mr. Harold Wagner.

119. *Magnolia Branch with Blossom*, 1908, watercolor on paper 14 x 11 (sight), dated bottom right.
Collection of The Oakland Museum (64.59.63),
Gift of Mr. Harold Wagner.

120. *Poster — Art Exhibition Sketch Club*, ink on paper 14¾ x 18⅜, signed bottom right. *Plate page 29.*
Collection of The Oakland Museum (65.13.203),
Gift of Concours d'Antiques, Art Guild, The Oakland Museum Association.

121. *Pink Cactus Blossom*, 1909, watercolor on paper 14 x 11 (sight), dated bottom right.
Collection of The Oakland Museum (64.59.69),
Gift of Mr. Harold Wagner.

122. *Magnolia Blossom*, watercolor on paper 12 x 11 (sight), dated with poppy monogram bottom center.
Collection of The Oakland Museum (64.59.65),
Gift of Mr. Harold Wagner.

123. *Portrait of Red-Haired Girl*, 1910, watercolor on paper 25½ x 18¼, signed bottom left. *Plate page 39.*
Frame: Furniture Shop; fruit and foliage design, carved and stained wood 41¼ x 34¼.
Collection of The Oakland Museum (64.59.140),
Gift of Mr. Harold Wagner.

124. *Monterey Cypress*, watercolor on paper 10 x 10 (sight), no signature.
Collection of The Oakland Museum (64.59.86),
Gift of Mr. Harold Wagner.

125. *Landscape with Oak Tree*, watercolor on paper 18¼ x 15¾ (sight), no signature.
Collection of The Oakland Museum (64.59.130),
Gift of Mr. Harold Wagner.

126. *Landscape with Mountain Road,* watercolor on paper 19½ x 23½ (sight), no signature.
Collection of The Oakland Museum (64.59.112),
Gift of Mr. Harold Wagner.

127. *Monterey Pine with Opium Poppies,* watercolor on paper 19½ x 23½, no signature. *Plate page 122.*
Collection of The Oakland Museum (64.59.124),
Gift of Mr. Harold Wagner.

128. *Valley Landscape,* watercolor on paper 19½ x 23½ (sight), no signature.
Collection of The Oakland Museum (64.59.113),
Gift of Mr. Harold Wagner.

129. *Monterey Coast,* watercolor on paper 10¾ x 14¾ (sight), signed bottom right.
Collection of The Oakland Museum (64.59.81),
Gift of Mr. Harold Wagner.

130. *Peony Calendar — January, 1921,* gouache and gold leaf on paperboard 9¼ x 8⅛, no signature.
Collection of The Oakland Museum (64.59.54),
Gift of Mr. Harold Wagner.

131. *Peony Calendar — 1921,* guoache and gold leaf on paperboard 9¼ x 8, signed bottom right.
Collection of The Oakland Museum (64.59.48),
Gift of Mr. Harold Wagner.

132. *Figures and Fruit Trees,* gouache and gold leaf on paper 6½ x 12½, no signature.
Collection of The Oakland Museum (65.13.187),
Gift of Concours d'Antiques, Art Guild, The Oakland Museum Association.

133. *Figure by Sea,* gouache, pencil, ink and gold leaf on paper 11 x 14⅞, no signature.
Collection of The Oakland Museum (65.13.186),
Gift of Concours d'Antiques, Art Guild, The Oakland Museum Association.

134. *California Poppies in Tall Goblet,* gouache, ink and gold leaf on paper 15⅝ x 11, no signature. *Plate page 75.*
Collection of The Oakland Museum (65.13.170),
Gift of Concours d'Antiques, Art Guild, The Oakland Museum Association.

135. *Design for Plate Border,* pencil and watercolor on paper 15⅛ x 15⅜, no signature.
Collection of The Oakland Museum (65.13.168),
Gift of Concours d'Antiques, Art Guild, The Oakland Museum Association.

136. *Portrait of Arthur F. Mathews,* watercolor on paper 11 x 10½, no signature. Frame: Furniture Shop; carved wood 22½ x 22.
Collection of The Oakland Museum (66.196.27),
Gift of Mr. Harold Wagner.

137. *Figure and Flowers Calendar — 1918,* gouache and gold leaf on paper 9⅞ x 8⅞, no signature.
Collection of The Oakland Museum (64.59.52),
Gift of Mr. Harold Wagner.

FURNITURE SHOP

138. Preliminary sketches and plans for furniture in the Masonic Temple, San Francisco, 1913, Arthur Mathews; actual size and scale drawings, pencil on paper.
Lent by The Masonic Temple Association of California, Inc., William C. Leeson, Secretary.

139. 4-Panel Screen, Lucia Mathews; magnolia design, painted and gold-leafed wood 72 x 80, no signature. *Plate page 74.*
Collection of The Oakland Museum (66.196.35),
Gift of Concours d'Antiques, Art Guild, The Oakland Museum Association.

140. Hexagonal Box with Lid, Lucia Mathews; floral designs, carved and painted wood 11½ x 6¾ diam., no signature. *Plate page 91.*
Collection of The Oakland Museum (66.196.37a,b),
Gift of Concours d'Antiques, Art Guild, The Oakland Museum Association.

141. Cabinet, Arthur and Lucia Mathews; poppy design panels, painted and incised wood 49¼ x 27½, no signature. *Plate page 87.*
Collection of The Oakland Museum (66.196.49),
Gift of Concours d'Antiques, Art Guild, The Oakland Museum Association.

142. 2 Chairs, Arthur F. Mathews; incised floral design, carved and stained wood 41½ x 23 x 20, no signature. *Plate page 74* (one chair shown)
Collection of The Oakland Museum (65.13.452 a,b),
Gift of Concours d'Antiques, Art Guild, The Oakland Museum Association.

143. Mirror, Lucia Mathews; floral design, painted wood 8½ diam., no signature.
Collection of The Oakland Museum (72.8.7),
Gift of Concours d'Antiques, Art Guild, The Oakland Museum Association.

144. Rectangular Box with Lid, Lucia Mathews; poppy designs, carved, gold-leafed and painted wood 3 x 7¾ x 4, no signature.
Collection of The Oakland Museum (66.196.42c),
Gift of Concours d'Antiques, Art Guild, The Oakland Museum Association.

145. Rectangular Box with Lid, 1929, Lucia Mathews; poppy design and panel landscapes, painted wood 5 x 16 x 12, signed on lid, bottom center. *Plate page 76.*
Collection of The Oakland Museum (66.196.42a),
Gift of Concours d'Antiques, Art Guild, The Oakland Museum Association.

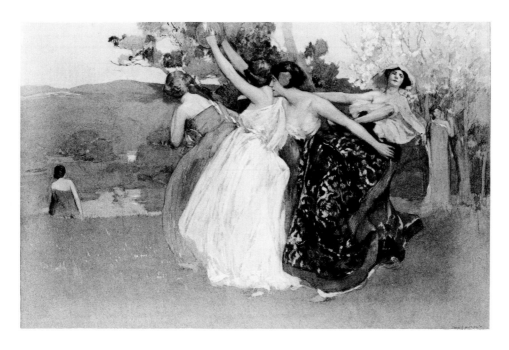

(Cat. no. 73)
Arthur F. Mathews
Dancing Figures, 1910

146. Rectangular Box with Lid, Lucia Mathews; figures in landscape, painted wood 3 x 12½ x 7¾, Furniture Shop hallmark stamped on bottom of box. *Plate page 85.*
   Collection of The Oakland Museum (66.196.42b),
   Gift of Concours d'Antiques, Art Guild, The Oakland Museum Association.

147. Baluster-shape Candlestick, Lucia Mathews; floral and figurative design, painted, gold-leafed and turned wood 22¼ x 8¼ diam., no signature.
   Collection of The Oakland Museum (66.196.36),   *Plate page 89.*
   Gift of Concours d'Antiques, Art Guild, The Oakland Museum Association.

148. Cylindrical Candlestick, Arthur and Lucia Mathews; floral and figurative design, painted, incised and turned wood 26¾ x 9 diam., no signature. *Plate page 91.*
   Collection of The Oakland Museum (66.196.48),
   Gift of Concours d'Antiques, Art Guild, The Oakland Museum Association.

149. Pair of Cylindrical Candlesticks, Arthur and Lucia Mathews; floral designs, carved, painted and turned wood 29½ x 7 diam., no signature. *Plate page 82.*
   Collection of The Oakland Museum (66.196.41a,b),
   Gift of Concours d'Antiques, Art Guild, The Oakland Museum Association.

150. Clock, Lucia Mathews; floral and figurative designs, gold-leafed and painted wood with electrical clock parts by Laterbury Clock Co. 14¾ x 6 x 4, signed on reverse. *Plate page 86*.
Collection of The Oakland Museum (66.196.31),
Gift of Concours d'Antiques, Art Guild, The Oakland Museum Association.

151. Hourglass, Arthur and Lucia Mathews; poppy design, carved and painted wood 9 x 5 diam., no signature. *Plate page 86*.
Collection of The Oakland Museum (66.196.53),
Gift of Concours d'Antiques, Art Guild, The Oakland Museum Association.

152. Wooden Jar with Lid, Arthur and Lucia Mathews; figures in landscape with floral borders, gold-leafed, painted and turned wood 11½ x 8 diam., no signature. *Plate page 26*.
Collection of The Oakland Museum (66.196.44 a,b),
Gift of Concours d'Antiques, Art Guild, The Oakland Museum Association.

153. Wooden Jar with Lid, Arthur and Lucia Mathews; floral border with glass bead finial on lid, painted and turned wood 6¾ x 5½ diam., no signature. *Plate page 87*.
Collection of The Oakland Museum (66.196.45 a,b),
Gift of Concours d'Antiques, Art Guild, The Oakland Museum Association.

154. Dining Table, 1918, Lucia Mathews; band of figures in landscape with floral borders, painted and gold-leafed wood 30 x 61 x 109¼, signed in side floral border.
Collection of The Oakland Museum (65.13.255),
Gift of Concours d'Antiques, Art Guild, The Oakland Museum Association.

155. Frame with Blue Glass Mirror, 1910, Arthur Mathews; classical and religious motifs with The Lord's Prayer incised, carved, painted and gold-leafed wood 91¾ x 63¼, stamped poppy hallmark bottom right.
Collection of The Oakland Museum (65.13.243),
Gift of Concours d'Antiques, Art Guild, The Oakland Museum Association.

156. Cylindrical Candlestick with Triangular Base, Arthur and Lucia Mathews; figurative and bird designs, carved, painted and turned wood 63¾ x 10 diam., no signature. *Plate page 74*.
Collection of The Oakland Museum (66.196.40),
Gift of Concours d'Antiques, Art Guild, The Oakland Museum Association.

157. Wooden Jar with Lid, Lucia Mathews; band of figures in landscape with landscape borders, lid with figures and animals in relief, carved, gold-leafed, painted aud turned wood 11½ x 11½ diam., no signature. *Plate pages 74, 82 and 87*.
Collection of The Oakland Museum (66.196.38 a,b),
Gift of Concours d'Antiques, Art Guild, The Oakland Museum Association.

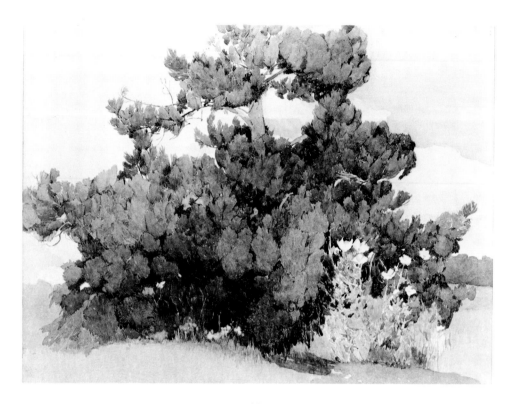

(Cat. no. 127)
Lucia K. Mathews
Monterey Pine with Opium Poppies

158. Chest, Arthur and Lucia Mathews; front and side panels of figures in landscape with drawer panels of floral and figurative designs, carved, painted and inlaid wood, scarab hardware, 46½ x 81 x 26½, no signature. *Plate page 82.*
Collection of The Oakland Museum (66.196.43),
Gift of Concours d'Antiques, Art Guild, The Oakland Museum Association.

159. Writing Table, Arthur and Lucia Mathews; floral and figurative designs, carved, incised and painted wood, scarab hardware, 30 x 44¾ x 22½, no signature. *Plate page 26.*
Collection of The Oakland Museum (66.196.29),
Gift of Concours d'Antiques, Art Guild, The Oakland Museum Association.

160. Panel, Lucia Mathews; figures in landscape with poppy and leaf borders, painted and gold-leafed wood 12¼ x 9½ x 5½, no signature. *Plate page 88.*
Lent by Mr. and Mrs. John Garzoli, San Francisco.

161. Footed Bowl, Lucia Mathews; medallions with Roman gods, grape and poppy borders, painted and turned wood 4½ x 7 diam., no signature.
Lent by Mr. and Mrs. John Garzoli, San Francisco.

162. Wooden Jar with Lid, Lucia Mathews; poppy designs, painted, gold-leafed and turned wood 5¾ x 5¾ diam., no signature. *Plate page 88.*
Lent by Mrs. Margaret R. Kleinhans, San Francisco.

163. Rectangular Box with Lid, 1916, Lucia Mathews; floral and figurative designs, painted wood 4¼ x 13 x 8½, dated on inside of lid.
Lent by Mrs. Margaret R. Kleinhans, San Francisco.

164. Wooden Jar with Lid, Lucia Mathews; band of figures in landscape, floral design panels, figures in landscape in relief on lid, 13 x 11¼ diam., signed in decorative band.
Lent by Mrs. Margaret R. Kleinhans, San Francisco.

165. Wooden Jar with Lid, Lucia Mathews; band of figures in landscape, painted, gold-leafed and turned wood 11½ x 8 diam., no signature.
Collection of The Oakland Museum (72.8.6 a-c),
Gift of the Concours d'Antique, Art Guild, The Oakland Museum Assn.

166. Desk, Arthur and Lucia Mathews; figures in landscape with medallions, borders and panels of figurative, floral and foliage designs; painting of female figure by Arthur F. Mathews on interior, back panel, scarab hardware 59 x 48 x 20, no signature. *Plate page 87.*
Collection of The Oakland Museum (72.8.5),
Gift of the Concours d'Antiques, Art Guild, The Oakland Museum Assn.

167. Desk, Arthur and Lucia Mathews; figures in landscape with medallions, borders and panels of figurative floral and foliage designs; seascape painting by Arthur F. Mathews on interior, back panel, scarab hardware 59 x 48 x 20, no signature.
Collection of The Oakland Museum (72.15),
Gift of Mrs. Margaret R. Kleinhans, San Francisco.

168. Side Table, Arthur F. Mathews; carved and stained wood 36 x 54 x 18¾, no signature.
Collection of The Oakland Museum (72.9.2),
Gift of Mr. and Mrs. J. R. Davison and Mr. and Mrs. R Henderson, Livermore.

169. Two chairs, Arthur Mathews; incised, carved and painted wood 39 x 19 x 19, with crest of the Sloss family, no signature.
Collection of The Oakland Museum (72.8.1),
Gift of Mr. and Mrs. J. R. Davison and Mr. and Mrs. R. Henderson, Livermore.

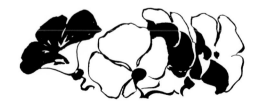

Ashe, Elizabeth H. *Intimate Letters from France During America's First Year of War.* San Francisco, Philopolis Press, 1918.
Bancroft Library; California State Library

Clarke, Dwight L. *The Passing of Pan: A Metrical Drama in a Prologue and Four Acts.* San Francisco, Philopolis Press, 1915.
California State Library; California Historical Society

Cornell, Hughes. *Dotty Seaweed.* With rhymes by Bertha Boye; copyright 1908 by Hughes Cornell; Philopolis Press mark, Advertisement for in *Philopolis* January 25, 1910.
California State Library

D'Estournelles de Constant, Baron. *Woman in the United States.* San Francisco, A. M. Robertson, 1912.
California Historical Society

Florine, Margaret Helen. *Songs of a Nurse.* San Francisco, Philopolis Press, 1917.
Bancroft Library

Irwin, Inez Haynes. *The Californiacs.* San Francisco, A. M. Robertson, 1916.
Bancroft Library, California Historical Society; California State Library; The Oakland Museum

Jordan, David Starr, and Kellogg, Vernon L. *The Scientific Aspects of Luther Burbank's Work.* San Francisco, A. M. Robertson, 1909.
Bancroft Library; California State Library

Kingsley, Charles. *The Pleasant Isle of Aves: To H. Morse Stephens.* San Francisco, 1907.
Bancroft Library

McAdie, Alexander. *The Clouds and Fogs of San Francisco.* San Francisco, A. M. Robertson, 1912. Decorations by Lucia K. Mathews; frontispiece by Arthur F. Mathews, Philopolis Series.
Bancroft Library; California Historical Society; California State Library; The Oakland Museum

McAdie, Alexander. *Infra Nubem, The Lights Outside, La Bocana.* San Francisco, A. M. Robertson, 1909. Decorations by Lucia K. Mathews; frontispiece by Arthur F. Mathews, Philopolis Series.
Bancroft Library

MacDonald, Augustin S., compiler. *A Collection of Verse by California Poets from 1849 to 1915.* San Francisco, A. M. Robertson, 1914.
Bancroft Library

McLaren, John. *Gardening in California, Landscape and Flower.* San Francisco, A. M. Robertson, 1909.
Bancroft Library; California State Library

Neuhaus, Eugen. *Painters, Pictures and the People.* San Francisco, Philopolis Press, 1918.
Bancroft Library; California State Library

Rowbins, James. *Impressions: California and the West: A Tribute to a Land of Deeds and Sunshine.* San Francisco, Privately printed, 1913.
California State Library

Ryder, Arthur William. *Women's Eyes: Being Verses Translated from the Sanskrit.* San Francisco, A. M. Robertson, 1917.
California Historical Society

Shurtleff, Ernest Warburton. *Songs on the Waters: Steamer Letter for Mrs. Morton Mitchell.* San Francisco, Privately printed, 1913.
Private Collection

Smith, Clark Ashton. *The Star-Treader and Other Poems.* San Francisco, A. M. Robertson, 1912.
Bancroft Library; California State Library

Steele, Rufus. *The City That Is: The Story of the Rebuilding of San Francisco in Three Years.* San Francisco, A. M. Robertson, 1909.
Bancroft Library; California State Library

Taussig, Hugo Alois. *Retracing the Pioneers: From West to East in an Automobile.* San Francisco, Privately printed, 1910.
Bancroft Library; California State Library

Philopolis, A Monthly Magazine. Published at 1717 California Street, San Francisco, California. Volume 1, 1906 through Volume X, 1916.

Mailing Cards, 3½″ x 5½″, 1913-1916. Color reproductions of Mathews paintings, printed by Philopolis, 1917. California Street, San Francisco, California. Subjects identified as: The Victorious Spirit; California; Monterey Pine; The Soil; The Grain; Nature; The Arts; Conquest; Resignation; Dancing Figures; The Ghost Story; Landscapes (2), untitled; Wall Panel, untitled; Decorations, untitled.

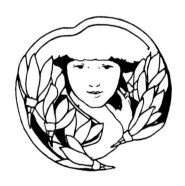

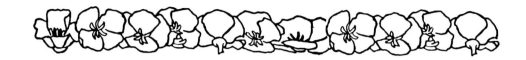

Index

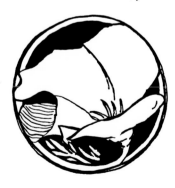

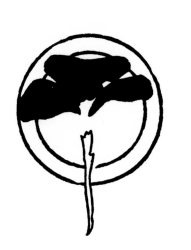

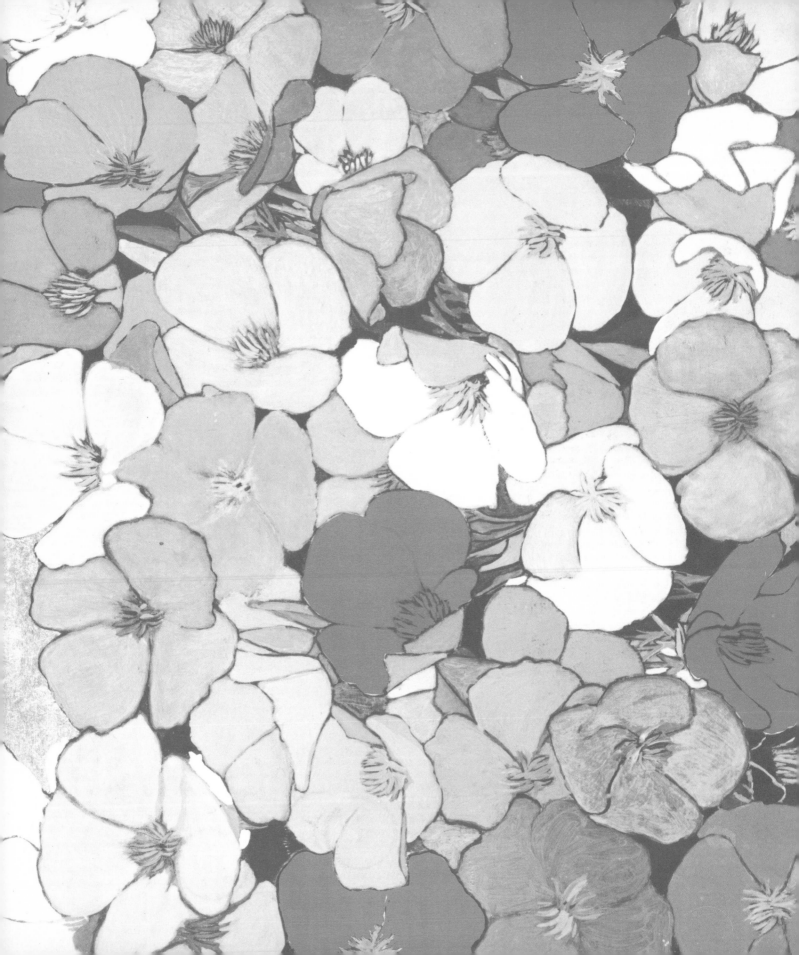